How to
Beat
Wall
Street

A Bit of Americana

About two years before the United States struck its first minted coins in the year 1792, America's first stock exchange began trading in Philadelphia. At that time throughout the Colonies, the Spanish-American doubloon, escudos, and pieces of eight were used as a medium of exchange.

The value of the doubloon was based upon the octol numeric system. One doubloon was worth eight gold escudos or sixteen pieces of eight. The octol numeric system was adopted with the trading of stocks denominated in $1/8$th or $1/16$. Today the stock exchanges still trade on the octol system, even though our coinage and dollars are based upon the decimal system.

How to
Beat
Wall
Street

*Trade to Win in
Stocks, Options
& Commodities*

Harold B. Wilson

LIBERTY HALL
PRESS™

LIBERTY HALL PRESS books are published by LIBERTY HALL PRESS, an imprint of McGraw-Hill, Inc. Its trademark, consisting of the words "LIBERTY HALL PRESS" and the portrayal of Benjamin Franklin, is registered in the United States Patent and Trademark Office.

FIRST EDITION
FIRST PRINTING

© 1991 by LIBERTY HALL PRESS, an imprint of McGraw-Hill, Inc.

Library of Congress Cataloging-in-Publication Data

Wilson, Harold B. (Harold Batting), 1910–
How to beat Wall Street : trade to win in stocks, options, and commodities / by Harold B. Wilson.
p.   cm.
Includes index.
ISBN 0-8306-3538-6 (h)
1. Stocks.   2. Options (Finance)   3. Commodity futures.
4. Speculation.   I. Title.
HG4661.W54   1990
332.63'22—dc20   90-49729
                                          CIP

For information about other McGraw-Hill materials,
call 1-800-2-MCGRAW in the U.S. In other countries
call your nearest McGraw-Hill office.

Questions regarding the content of this book should be addressed to:

Reader Inquiry Branch
LIBERTY HALL PRESS
Blue Ridge Summit, PA 17294-0850

Vice President and Editorial Director: David J. Conti
Book Editor: Joanne M. Slike
Production: Katherine G. Brown
Book Design: Jaclyn J. Boone

Contents

*To the millions of investors who make our
economic system and way of life the best
in the world and who are able to meet
the challenge of Wall Street*

Acknowledgments

The Author acknowledges and thanks the following for permission to reprint:

AMERICAN STOCK EXCHANGE
86 Trinity Place
New York City, NY 10006

B.C.A. PUBLICATIONS, LTD.
The Bank Credit Analyst
3463 Peel Street
Montreal, Quebec,
Canada H3A 1W7

CORE INDUSTRIES INC
500 North Woodward
P.O. Box 2000
Bloomfield Hills, MI 48013

SECURITIES RESEARCH COMPANY
A Division of Babson-United
Investment Advisors, Inc.
208 Newbury Street
Boston, MA 02116

HOLLY WILSON – PERROTTO
7235 Canton Street
Baldwinsville, NY 13027

About This Book

COMPRESSED INTO THE PAGES OF THIS BOOK, THE READER WILL FIND a lifetime of knowledge acquired from a hands-on involvement in the financial markets.

How to Beat Wall Street: Trade to Win in Stocks, Options, and Commodities identifies numerous influences that signal when to enter or exit the markets, as well as many factors that disclose the strengths and weaknesses of companies whose stocks are traded on the exchanges.

Because most stocks decline in bear markets and rise in bull markets, the subject of technical considerations that influence movements in the stock market is presented in chapter 1.

Chapters 2 and 3 cover fundamental analysis and other factors to be considered in investment decisions. In addition, chapter 3 includes a study of 480 different "time cycles" that have occurred since 1930, and contains summary probabilities of relative strength in the stock market in the years 1990 through 1999 based upon these cycles.

Chapter 4 offers a detailed presentation concerning the term *percent return on equity*. It downgrades the implied value associated with such a term and warns against giving undue importance to it when considering a stock for purchase.

Chapter 5 provides strategies for consideration by short-term stock traders as distinguished from evaluative analyses used by long-term investors.

Chapter 6 furnishes an explanation of the terms used in trading of stock options. It highlights the risks involved in such trading and offers principles to follow that give traders a better edge than is found in most option trades.

Chapter 7 is devoted to trading in commodities. It specifies the importance of "charting" to determine when to enter or exit a futures contract. Chapter 7 points out the potential advantages in considering the changes in open interest as a factor in timing the purchase or sale of contracts.

How to Beat Wall Street was written to be used in three ways:

1. A first reading of the book will bring an insight into the financial markets; 2. Additional perusals will infuse the reader with knowledge of forces that move the markets and with the characteristics of companies that can identify stocks and other financial instruments for possible purchase or sale; 3. Making continuing reference to the book will bring reminders of factors and influences, as well as strategies to employ, which should enhance the making of successful investment decisions by investors.

Introduction

Historical Background of the Stock Market

THE STOCK MARKET IS A PLACE WHERE PEOPLE PIT THEIR WITS against one another in quest of financial gain . . . a place where people have made great fortunes and others are still waiting . . . a place where vast sums have been lost . . . a place where, within the heart of all, glows a never-ending desire for profit . . . a place where there are others who are always ready to accept your challenge.

Where and when did the stock exchange originate? It all began in the early 1790s on Wall Street, those few short blocks with a river at one end and a graveyard at the other. A group of entrepreneurs would meet daily and execute buy and sell orders for the public in the few issues that were available. A number of years later, the Tontine Coffee House was built and occupied by the counterparts of our modern-day brokers.

The constitution of the stock exchange was adopted in 1817. Among other things, it provided that each day at 11:30 A.M., the president of the exchange would call out the stocks offered for sale. It wasn't until the early 1870s that the morning call list market succumbed to a continuous one. In 1886 a single day's trading volume exceeded 1,000,000 shares for the first time. (To give you an idea of how much the stock market has expanded since those early days, consider a few figures: On June 21, 1968, 21,350,000 shares were traded; on October 18, 1968, 7,660,000 shares were traded in the first hour; and on October 19, 1987 over 500,000,000 shares were traded in a deluge of selling!)

The present stock exchange building on Broad and Wall Streets was built in 1903. The exchange did not have a paid president until 1938.

The American Stock Exchange did not have as early a beginning as the New York Stock Exchange. Its predecessor first began trading in the mid-1880s. Hanover Street, near Wall Street, was the first "Curb" site. In stages, the market outgrew narrower confines and drifted toward aptly named Broad Street, south of Wall, where there was more room.

It was here at the beginning of the twentieth century that trading by the outdoor brokers became more organized. In 1908 a small group of them formed the New York Curb Agency. By 1911 the Agency had evolved into the New York Curb Market Association with offices at 6 Wall Street. Trading rules were drawn up and a listing department created.

Until then, the Curb Market had operated without formal rules or supervision. There were, of course, no requirements to become a broker, though a booming voice and a strong constitution helped.

The heyday of the outdoor market occurred during and immediately after World War I. Much of the trading was in "war brides": steel, munitions, coppers, and marine stocks. Brokers overflowed the curbs on Broad Street at Exchange Place, just south of the *Wall Street Journal* office. Elbow to elbow, and sometimes nose to nose, they jammed the street, tying up both pedestrian and vehicular traffic. By this time telephone order clerks were a common sight, sitting astride window ledges along Broad Street, communicating with the crowd of brokers in a one-hand sign language.

The brokers in the street crowd took to wearing distinctive clothing so that they might be identified more readily by their telephone clerks. On their heads were all sorts of hats—bowlers, boaters, caps, fedoras, homburgs—in bright colors such as red and green; some also had special markings. A lamppost served as a place to list the securities being traded.

NEITHER SNOW NOR RAIN . . .

No fair-weather crowd was this. They met year-round and were proud of their reputation for hardiness. When a 10-inch rainstorm hit New

York City on October 8 and 9, 1903, and turned some of its streets into rivers, it is said that only ducks and Curb brokers weathered the storm. Clad in rubber coats and fishermen's hoods, the traders kept at their business.

Even prolonged sub-zero weather, as in February of 1918, when the temperature dropped to 13 degrees below zero, could not stall them.

In 1919, with volume mounting and public interest becoming more widespread, the New York Curb Market Association decided to move indoors to a site a few blocks west of Broad Street and Exchange Place. The formal opening on Trinity Place, behind the venerable Trinity Church, occurred on June 27, 1921.

Some of the outdoor brokers who were not members of the Association remained diehards. They continued to trade at the old stand, making a secondary market in listed securities. This activity eventually diminished, and traffic began to move again on Broad Street.

On January 5, 1953 the term "Curb" itself gave way to modernity when that exchange became the American Stock Exchange.

* * *

Today there are over thirty million stockholders in the United States with stocks of about 2000 companies traded on the New York Stock Exchange alone. Stock advisers, brokers, and analysts abound!

Mostly the analysts and advisers of today employ what is generally referred to as *technical analysis* or *fundamental analysis* in formulating their recommendations for the purchase or sale of securities.

The elements comprising fundamental analysis are distinct and mutually exclusive of those of technical analysis. Yet, almost daily there are some individuals who express their views via the financial media and indiscriminately and erroneously intermix fundamental analysis with technical analysis. Unfortunately, the public often relies upon their views.

How, then, under these conditions, can a person beat Wall Street? The answer is to become knowledgeable of the elements comprising both fundamental and technical analysis and to apply the *best* features of each when making investment decisions. After reading this book, I hope you will agree it is not as difficult as it seems.

1

Technical Analysis and Stock Market Strategy

WHEN YOU ACQUIRE KNOWLEDGE IN ANY FIELD OF ENDEAVOR, YOU ARE fortified with a major ingredient for success. When you learn how and when to make proper use of that knowledge, opportunity for success becomes enhanced. So, even after acquiring a wealth of knowledge, you must determine a plan of action to put such valuable knowledge to use.

A game plan for investing in the stock market should embrace the following considerations:

1. Often only a single clear-cut technical signal is required to foretell a change in market direction as a whole. If several signals flash simultaneously, so much the better.

2. Before any investment action is taken, it is best to use fundamental analysis to search out positive and negative factors regarding an individual company—then weigh these factors against each other. Only when there is a preponderance of positive over negative factors should you earmark a stock for potential purchase.

3. Even when a particular stock purchase appears warranted, you should look at technical analysis signals to determine whether

1

the "timing" appears favorable for entry into the stock market.

4. When you are "out of the market," you should do your homework by following steps 1 through 3. This will provide you with a listing of potential stock purchases of specific companies. In addition, you should devote a half hour's time each week perusing *Barron's Weekly*. This way, you will always be in a position to:

   a. enter the market again when one or more technical buy signals flash, or . . .
   b. exit the market when one or more technical sell signals flash.

5. Be sure to use the "value ratings," provided in chapters 1 and 2, that are technical and fundamental factors.

6. In applying steps 1 through 5 as a basic investment philosophy, you will find that during many periods of varying duration you will either be out of the market completely or mostly invested.

   NOTE: A word of caution here: Being 100% invested should be avoided. Also, for the ordinary investor, buying on margin is not recommended. Such positions do not allow for leeway; sudden market moves in the wrong direction can result in adverse psychological reaction. Under trying conditions, buying on margin and being more than 100% invested precludes possible alternatives. At worst, it can be devastating.

   An alternative to being 100% invested would be to have a maximum of 75% of investment funds (exclusive of insurance and real estate) in equities; 20% in T. notes or Bills or Money Market Funds; and 5% in gold coins and silver coins or bars. This distribution allows flexibility when additional action is necessary.

7. If you find yourself out of the market, it is best to reenter it on a piecemeal basis. When the technical signals say "go," and you have a fairly updated potential stock purchase list, it may prove prudent to initially invest, say, 20% of your investment funds. Then, if the technical "buy" signal was wrong, you will have an option to use available funds, as suggested by some investment advisers, or to "average down," by investing the same dollar amount as the original purchase of the stock. However, there is disagreement among investment advisors concerning this practice. A majority of investment advisers believe

it best to cut losses short and let profits run. This view has often proved to be preferable.

In the event the stocks move up in price you might want to "average up" in the same amount as in the original investment; or, if you believe the stock has reached a suitable price, you can place a stop order on the shares of stock to lock in profits. If the price continues to rise, you should keep raising your stop order. If the price of the stock drops to the stop-loss price or on the next trade below that price, the stock will automatically be sold. This way, greed, which has far too often caused ultimate grief or worse, can never come into play.

* * *

Because most stocks rise in price in a bull market and fall in a bear market, it is of paramount importance to continually observe technical factors, which often signal when to enter or exit the stock market. On a "timing" basis, the subject of technical analysis should be given first consideration.

TECHNICAL ANALYSIS IN HISTORY

Many signals that affect the stock market have had a direct influence on action taken by investors over a period of many decades. Long ago, one such successful investor was Hetty Green, also known as "The Witch of Wall Street."

In the spring of 1907 money had become scarce and stock prices began to fall. On March 14th of that year the Panic of 1907 began. Stocks dropped from 10% to 25% of their value in that one day alone!

In February 1908, Hetty Green, the second-richest woman in the United States, was interviewed by a reporter of the *Boston Traveler* about the Panic of 1907:

I saw this situation developing three years ago, and I am on record as predicting it. I said then that the rich were approaching the brink, and that a "panic" was inevitable.

There were signs which I couldn't ignore. Some of the solidest men of the "street" came to me and wanted to unload all sorts of things, from palatial residences to automobiles. The New York Central quietly negotiated with me for a big loan, and that made me sit up and do some thinking; for that road is one of the wealthiest in the world.

There had been an enormous inflation of values, and when the unloading process was begun the holders of the securities found great difficulty in getting real money from the public. The stringency was felt by the big brokers and manipulators long before the people had any inkling that such a condition existed.

I saw the handwriting on the wall and began quietly to call in my money, making few new transactions and getting into my hands every dollar of my fortune against the day I knew was coming. Every real-estate deal which I could possibly close up was converted into cash. I never buy real estate. First mortgages are good enough for me.

When the crash came I had money, and I was one of the very few who really had it. The others had their "securities" and their "values." I had the cash, and they had to come to me.

Fig. 1-1. Brokers trading on Broad Street circa 1905. (Courtesy of American Stock Exchange)

The views expressed by Hetty Green in 1908 could have been written a number of times over the years. For instance, weren't her concerns again prevalent prior to the great crash of 1929? Didn't the same fears of tight money and inflation exist in 1972 prior to the drop of nearly 500 points in the Dow Industrials in 1973 and 1974? Wasn't avarice coming to full bloom during the parabolic rise in the market prior to the one-day crash of over 500 points (18%) on October 19, 1987?

Each event above, of course, represents unusual circumstances. It should also be recognized that dozens of less dramatic moves, both up and down, have provided opportunities to profit in the stock market.

Certainly all these moves in the market underscore the need of today's investor to be aware of fundamental factors and technical influences in making their investment decisions.

TECHNICAL ANALYSIS DEFINED

Technical analysis (TA) makes use of numerous factors, occurrences, or influences of the outside world that may have an impact on the stock market as a whole as well as on the price movements of individual stocks. To further elaborate, let's look at a few well-known TA signals.

A DISCOUNT RATE TURNAROUND COINCIDING WITH A TRIGGERED DOW THEORY SIGNAL— A Classic Technical Analysis Buy Signal

Changes in the discount rate have often had a significant effect on the stock market. The discount rate is the fee charged by the twelve Federal Reserve District Banks (Boston, San Francisco, Richmond, Chicago, Kansas City, Philadelphia, Cleveland, St. Louis, Minneapolis, Dallas, Atlanta, and New York City) on loans made to member commercial banks.

History tells us that on a number of occasions the Federal Reserve followed the practice of raising the discount rate when the economy seemed to be heating up and the Dow Industrials was reaching a high point. The Federal Reserve also has lowered the rate when it seemed the Dow Industrials was at a relatively low point and the economy needed stimulation.

When the Dow Industrials hit a high of 1067 in January 1973, the Federal Reserve began a series of seven consecutive increases in the discount rate, which tightened the money supply. By December 1974 the Dow Industrials had dropped 497 points, from 1067 to a low of 570. At that time a Dow Theory buy signal was also triggered.

THE DOW THEORY

The Dow Theory flashes a buy signal when the Dow Industrial average hits a new low that is not confirmed with a new low in the Dow Transportation Average. Contrawise, it flashes a sell signal when the Industrials hit a new high that is not confirmed by the Transportation Average. (See Figs. 1-2 and 1-3.)

COMBINATION OF DISCOUNT RATE TURNAROUND AND THE DOW THEORY SIGNAL

In September 1974 the Dow Industrial Average, the S&P 500, the Dow Transportation Average, the NYSE Composite, and the Dow Utilities Average all hit new lows. Two months later the Dow Industrials tested its previous low and went slightly below it. This drop by the Industrials below its previous low was, however, not confirmed by any of the other four averages, giving the Dow Theory buy signal.

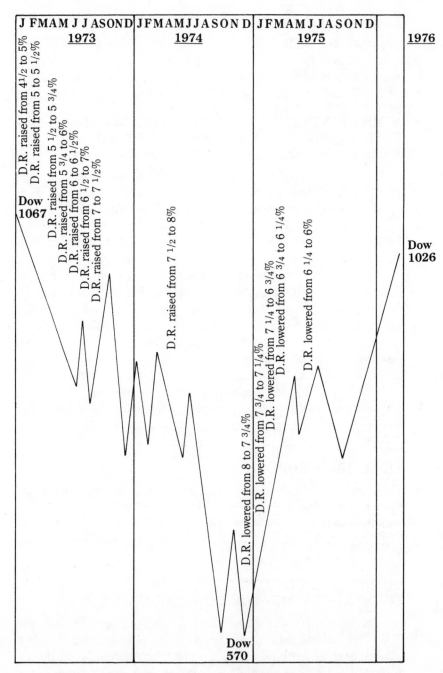

Fig. 1-2. Chart of Discount Rate Changes

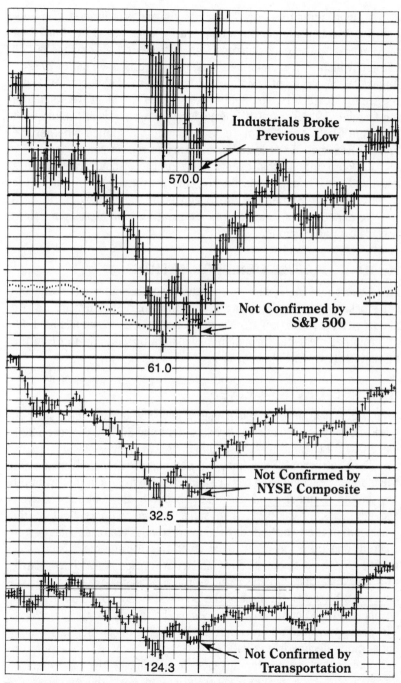

Fig. 1-3. Dow Not Confirmed: Often Portends a Change in Market Direction
(Chart Courtesy of Securities Research Company, labels added by author)

A month after the Dow Theory buy signal was flashed, the Federal Reserve began a series of consecutive decreases in the discount rate. Whether these concurrent signals triggered an enormous bull market, which with tremendous gusto reached a new high of 2722 in August 1987, two months before the great crash of October 19, 1987, is open to debate. Also, on September 4, 1987, and four weeks before the October 19, 1987 crash, the Federal Reserve raised the discount rate from $5^{1}/2\%$ to 6%. For years it may be questioned whether the Federal Reserve was at least contributory to that crash.

Yet keep in mind that events following the discount rate changes and the Dow Theory signal do not always evolve as they did in the above situations. Sometimes these signals are followed by events contrary to expectations. Such events are pleasing to numerous investors with contrarian opinions.

HEAD AND SHOULDERS FORMATIONS

Head and shoulder signals can be important in determining when to sell stocks or when an up-move in the stock market is anticipated. An almost perfect formation signalling when to sell is shown in Fig. 1-4.

Another clear-cut formation signalling a possible up-move in the market is shown in Fig. 1-5.

ADVANCE-DECLINE LINES

Many technical analysts make use of advance-decline lines in their work. Some use 20-day lines, while others use 30-, 40-, or even 200-day lines. All lines are established in a similar manner.

To construct a 20-day line, the number of stocks advancing and the number declining each day are added for 20 days. On the twentieth day the total number of advances are divided by 20 to obtain the average advances for 20 days. The same is done with respect to the declines. On the twentieth day the average advance or decline is subtracted, one from the other. That gives the average net advances or declines for the previous 20 days, and a dot is placed on a chart relative to a reference line. On the twenty-first and successive days the volume of advances on the first of the 20 days is deducted from the total advances and the number of advances on the twenty-first day is added. The same principle and procedure applies to the declines. Thus a moving advance-decline line is established.

The analyst relates the advance-decline line to the movement of its relative average market price trend line to see if the two lines are moving in harmony or whether a divergence exists. Figure 1-6 shows

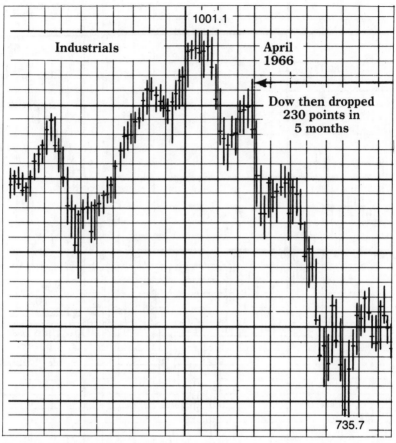

1001.1

Industrials

April
1966

Dow then dropped
230 points in
5 months

735.7

Fig. 1-4. Head and Shoulders Bearish Signal (Chart Courtesy of Securities Research Company, labels added by author)

the relationship between several different advance-decline lines relative to the movement in their respective market price averages. When the direction of the trend of both the advance-decline line and its related market price line is in agreement, it is viewed as a continuing sign of the direction of the market line. When not in agreement, it points to a possible change in direction of the market.

CORRELATION BETWEEN PRICE
TRENDS AND VOLUME SIGNAL

For many years technical analysts have studied charts showing price and volume trends, which has led many to believe that a correlation between the volume of transactions and the price trend of stocks exists.

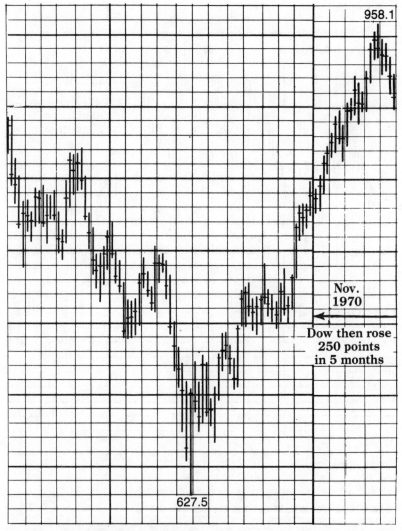

Fig. 1-5. Reverse Head and Shoulders Bullish Signal (Chart Courtesy of Securities Research Company, labels added by author)

The correlation between the movement of prices and volume trends seems to validate the old theory of supply and demand. Once an upward move in price has reached an apex and a down-trend begins that is accompanied by decreasing volume, it means more shares are being offered for sale than are being sought. Finally, a low point in volume is reached that often signals a drying up of the sell orders.

When the volume of stocks being sought outnumbers the volume of shares offered for sale, an uptrend begins. Thus, the broad-span

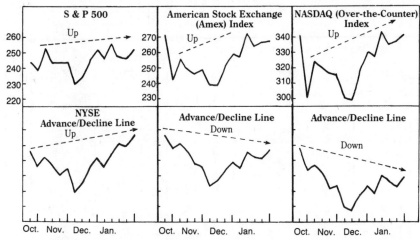

Fig. 1-6. Divergencies in Advance Decline Lines May Signal a Change in Market Trend from October 1987 to January 1988 (Courtesy of BCA Publications Ltd.)

movement of stock prices up and down and down and up is ever extant.

Notice in Figs. 1-7 and 1-8 the number of instances when volume decreased and prices decreased, and when volume increased and prices increased. Particularly of note is the frequency of up-points in the market, matched with tops in volume, and down-points, matched with lows in volume.

In addition, Fig. 1-8 represents a review of history that is akin to Monday-morning quarterbacking. It is one thing to observe action that has taken place and say, "Ah, that was the bottom . . . I could have bought there," and quite another to be able to pinpoint a bottom as the market is in motion. Observing the market movement in real time, couldn't it drop another 100 points or more before a bottom is reached?

Notwithstanding the high and low points in the market, no one has been able to consistently buy at the bottom and sell at the top. In fact, when asked how he acquired his millions, Bernard Barauch said, "I made my fortune by buying too soon and selling too late." He knew, however, that enough span existed between a cut from the bottom and a cut from the top in which to make money.

Modern-day technical analysts believe the same as Mr. Barauch. They know that in science it requires more force to slow or reverse movement than it takes to continue its propulsion. So, why not wait for such a force to exert itself and for the turnaround to actually occur and still buy at a cut from the bottom and sell at a cut from the top?

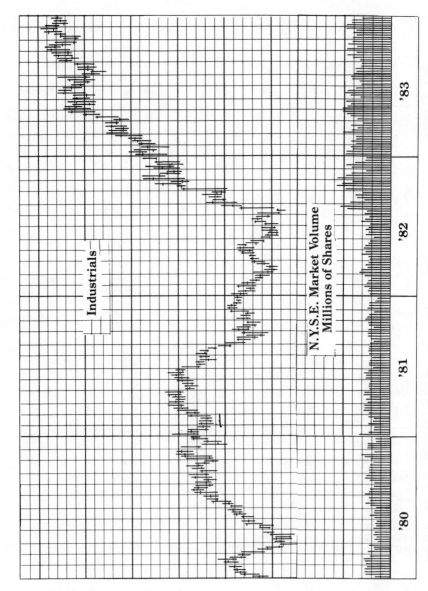

Industrials

N.Y.S.E. Market Volume
Millions of Shares

'80 '81 '82 '83

Fig. 1-7. Correlation Between Price Trends and Volume Signal (Chart Courtesy of Securities Research Company)

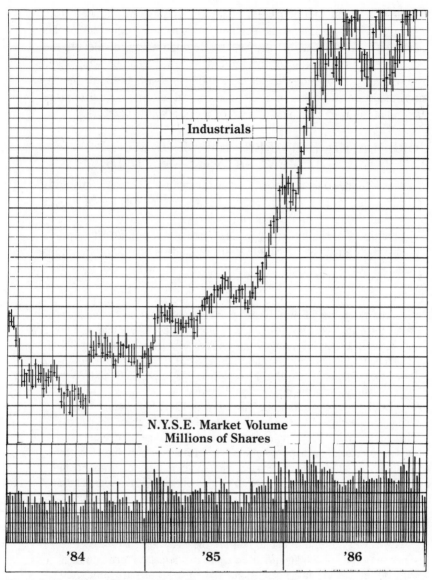

Fig. 1-8. Correlation Between Price Trends and Volume Signal (Chart Courtesy of Securities Research Company)

Now, it might well be asked: "After a turning point, how far from the top and bottom should the sell and buy spots be triggered?" This must be a judgment call by the investor. He must always be alert to the fact that even after a market turnaround occurs, he can be whipsawed by a reverse action. A risk factor in investing is always present. Investment made on the basis of a single technical analysis signal is more risky than investment based on two or more favorable factors.

CORRELATION BETWEEN VOLUME OF STOCKS AND PRICE MOVEMENT—A Twenty-Year-Old Study

"As it was then, so as it is now, and as it shall be." These words aptly describe the venerable correlation between the volume of stocks traded and the price movement of stocks.

In support of the longevity of this correlation, and for the readers who are mathematically inclined, a study made some 20 years ago is presented here.

* * *

The charts on the following pages point up what appears to be short-term correlations between volume and price trends. There may also be similar correlations between volume and price trends over the long pull. The following data relating to the volume of transactions on the American Stock Exchange and the price movements in Standard and Poors 425 Industrial Averages may prove of interest.

In 27 of the 42 years from 1926 through 1967, Standard and Poors Industrial Averages were higher at the end of the year than at the start. In 20 of these 27 years, the American Stock Exchange volume of transactions increased over the volume of the previous year. In the 15 of the 42 years in which prices declined, the Amex volume of transactions declined in 13 years, compared with volume of the previous year. There were only 2 years in the total of 42 in which the year's volume of transactions increased over the previous year while prices in those 2 years declined! The years: 1929 and 1966.

Following is an attempt to convert the following charted correlations between volume and price trends to mathematical terms to identify the extent of such correlations and their recurrence probability factor.

I supplied data to a mathematician friend of mine covering the extent of the extremes in high and low trends of volume and prices covering the period from November 3, 1966 through September 4, 1968. Table 1-1 on pp. 16 and 17 shows such volumes and prices in columns 1 and 2, respectively. The differentials of volumes and prices between associated high and low trends appear in columns 3 and 4. (Refer to Figs. 1-9 and 1-10.)

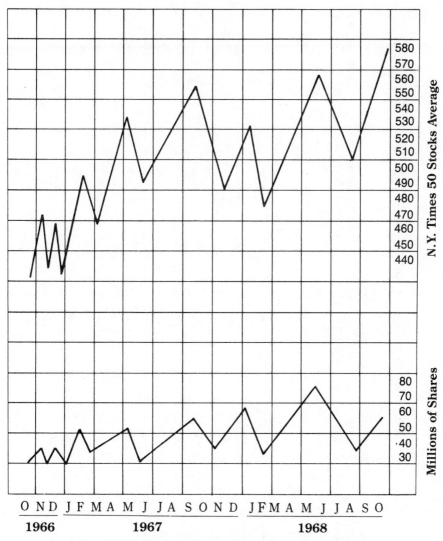

Fig. 1-9. Volume vs. Prices Shows Significant Correlation

The volume differentials were summed and divided by the number of the sample (36) to arrive at an average change "in volume" of $0.05(\bar{x})$. Likewise, the price differentials were summed and divided by 36 to arrive at an average change "in price" of $2.6(\bar{y})$. These figures were used in conjunction with the differentials to obtain the necessary ingredients for calculating the *coefficient of correlation, line of regression,* and the *standard error of estimate.* (These techniques can be found in most books on statistical analysis.)

Table 1-1 Changes in Volume and Prices

Transactions Volume (in millions)	Price (N.Y. Times 50 Stocks)	Change in Transaction Volume (in Millions)	No. of Points Change in Price (N.Y. Times 50 Stocks)	Change in Volume minus Average	Change in Price minus Average
40	475	xxx			
28	449	-12	-26	-12.5	-28.6
41	471	13	22	12.5	19.4
33	445	-8	-26	-8.5	-28.6
53	480	20	35	19.5	32.4
28	450	-25	-30	-25.5	-32.6
53	496	25	46	24.5	43.4
38	486	-15	-10	-15.5	-12.6
56	510	18	24	17.5	21.4
37	507	-19	-3	-19.5	-5.6
53	537	16	30	15.5	27.4
40	489	-13	-48	-13.5	-50.6
54	543	14	54	13.5	51.4
33	503	-21	-40	-21.5	-42.6
55	526	22	23	21.5	20.4
36	514	-19	-12	-19.5	-14.6
60	552	24	38	23.5	35.4
37	520	-23	-32	-23.5	-34.6

	Average Change (Volume)		(Price)		
x	y			(x − x̄)	(y − ȳ)
59	563	22	43	21.5	40.4
50	541	−9	−22	−9.5	−24.6
51	553	1	12	.5	9.4
42	497	−9	−56	−9.5	−58.6
60	527	18	30	17.5	27.4
49	514	−11	−13	−11.5	−15.6
66	534	17	20	16.5	17.4
34	485	−32	−49	−32.5	−51.6
50	500	16	15	15.5	12.4
41	486	−9	−14	−9.5	−16.6
78	520	37	34	36.5	31.4
47	509	−31	−11	−31.5	−13.6
73	556	26	47	25.5	44.4
54	529	−19	−27	−19.5	−29.6
82	560	28	31	27.5	28.4
39	530	−43	−30	−43.5	−37.6
69	559	30	29	29.5	26.4
38	529	−31	−30	−31.5	−32.6
59	570	21	41	20.5	38.4

$\bar{x}$ 0.5 $\bar{y}$ 2.6

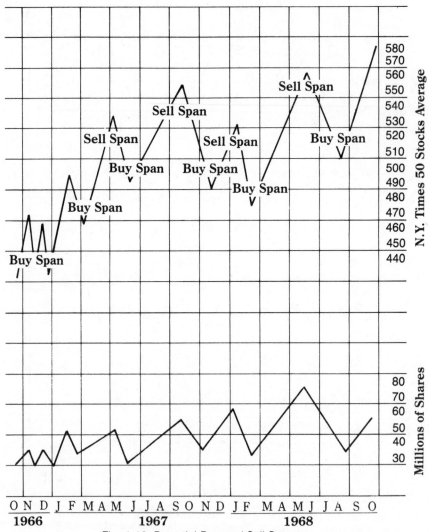

Fig. 1-10. Potential Buy and Sell Spans

The coefficient of correlation, based on actual data, was found to be .87, as compared to a perfect theoretical correlation of 1.0. (See Fig. 1-11.) From this it seems reasonable to state that during a trend, an increase in the volume of transactions will generally cause a corresponding increase in the price (to the extent researched we know of two exceptions, i.e., 1929 and 1966, as previously discussed), and conversely a decrease in the volume will generally cause a decrease in the price.

$$\text{Coefficient of Correlation} = \frac{\Sigma\,(X - \overline{X})\,(Y - \overline{Y})}{\sqrt{\Sigma\,(X - \overline{X})^2\Sigma\,\,\Sigma\,(Y - \overline{Y})^2}} = .87$$

$$b = \frac{\Sigma\,(X - Y)(Y - \overline{Y})}{\Sigma\,(X - \overline{Y})^2} = 1.3 \qquad a = \overline{Y} - b\overline{X} = 2.0$$

$$Y = bx + a$$

Change in No. of points in price = (1.3)
Change in transaction volume in millions = 2.0

Fig. 1-11. Coefficient of Correlation of Stock Prices and Volume

The line of regression is shown in Fig. 1-12 on p. 20. The formula for the regression line is y = 1.3x + 2, i.e., the change in price equals 1.3 times the change in volume (in millions) plus an equalization factor of 2. For example, if the weekly volume increased by 20 million shares, the change in price should equal 1.3(20) + 2 or rise by 28 points. This value could also be determined by following the regression line (solid) to the point where the change in volume equals 20, and then reading the corresponding vertical value (change in price). In the above example the value is shown by the circled point on the chart.

The dotted lines on the chart mark off one standard deviation (*standard error of estimate*) on either side of the regression line. Statistically speaking, 68% of the estimates of price differential (given a volume differential) will fall within the two dotted lines. Using the previous example, we can say that the increase in price will be between 12 and 44 points. Although this seems like a rather large spread, it should be noted that at least it represents an increase. Looking further at the chart, two facts are clearly patent. The first is that only 7 observed points are outside the area bounded by the dotted lines; in other words, 80% of the points are within our calculated range. The second fact is that no point is present in either the upper-left or lower-right quadrant of the chart, demonstrating that for the observed values not once was an increase in volume associated with a decrease in price, or decrease in volume accompanied by an increase in price. It must be noted, however, that this charting covered only a 2-year period and we know exceptions occurred in 1929 and 1966 on the downside. Also, this study is subject to one or more possible anomolies (not researched) in the interim years.

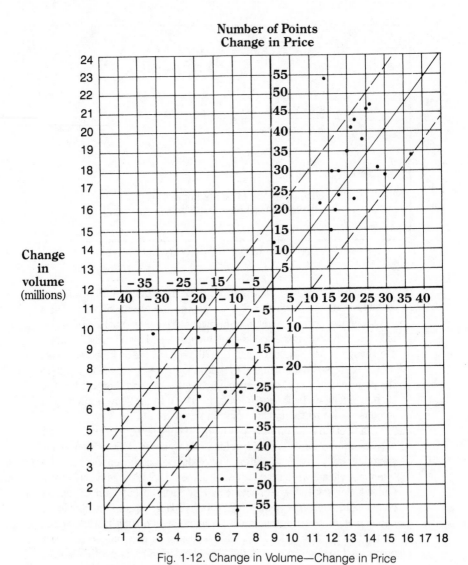

Fig. 1-12. Change in Volume—Change in Price

PUT-CALL RATIO—
A Contrary Opinion Sentiment Indicator

A number of well-known technical analysts use the put and call ratios as contrary sentiment indicators. Their belief is: 1. A high volume of put options in relation to the volume of call options is bullish; and 2. A low volume of put options compared with the volume of call options is bearish.

Thus, some technical analysts believe a change in the direction of the stock market is signalled when the following ratios occur:

	S&P 100				CBOE		
	Ratio				Ratio		
	Puts		*Calls*		*Puts*		*Calls*
Bullish →	70	to	100	Bullish→	65	to	100
Bearish →	30	to	100	Bearish→	30	to	100

INSIDER SELL-BUY RATIO

Figure 1-13 shows that, except for the insider peak in selling in December 1982 and again in 1986, the insider preponderance of sales was a good leading indicator of the market; whereas their low sales to buys ratio was an excellent barometer.

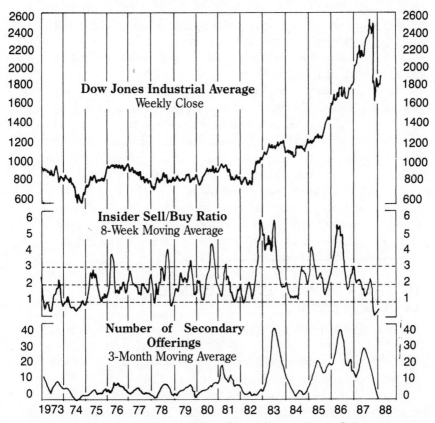

Fig. 1-13. Insider Sell-Buy Ratio May Signal Time to Buy or Sell (Courtesy of BCA Publications Ltd.)

WILL THE OCTOBER 1987 CRASH FOLLOW THE PATTERN OF THE OCTOBER 1929 DEBACLE?

Two great crashes in Wall Street occurred in the month of October: one on the 28th of 1929, the second on the 19th in 1987.

The first great crash was followed by several up and down moves. Then a gradual rising trend began and ended in the third week in April 1930, some six months after October 28, 1929. Soon a long stock market drop started that brought with it the Great Depression.

We should note that subsequent to the bull market of the twenties and the 1929 market crash, the bottom of the market was not reached until the middle of 1932, with the Dow Industrials then at 40.6. The Dow did not again reach its 1929 high of 381.17 until the year 1955, some 23 years later.

As this is written in May of 1990, the Dow Industrials has raged ahead to new all-time highs. At what point the peak will occur few, if any, stock market advisers can precisely predict. Yet, when storm winds begin blowing, certain signals discussed in these pages will begin to flash red. When two or more occur simultaneously, it is prudent to batten down the hatches.

Figure 1-14 shows the Dow Industrials pattern for the period between September 1987 through January 1988, and compares it with the pattern for the period between August 1929 through April 1930. These lines are followed by the 86% decline line. The table below the chart furnishes statistics of previous bear markets. As you'll note that in the past 69 years the average length of bear markets has been 19 months with several lasting over 30 months.

It is unpleasant to comment upon the above types of stock markets so, as an uplift, let's view what has happened in the market in presidential election years. Keep in mind that there will be five more election years before the year 2011.

THE STOCK MARKET IN PRESIDENTIAL ELECTION YEARS

Some technical analysts consider the stock market behavior in past presidential election years as guidelines for action in future years. Table 1-2 reflects the high and low points in the Dow Industrials during the past 17 presidential election years.

Note that in 14 of the 17 years the Dow Industrials hit its lows during the first half of the year, while the highs were reached in November and December in eight of the 17 years. Also worthy of note is that since the year 1916, there has never been two consecutive

Dow Jones Industrial Average: 1929 and 1987 – 1988

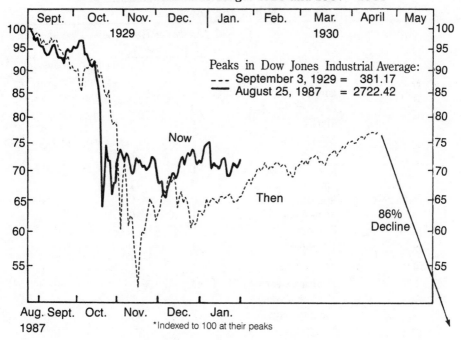

Peaks in Dow Jones Industrial Average:
--- September 3, 1929 =   381.17
— August 25, 1987   = 2722.42

Now

Then

86% Decline

Aug. Sept. Oct.   Nov.   Dec.   Jan.
1987   *Indexed to 100 at their peaks

Past Bear Markets

Date	Length (Months)	% Loss in DJIA
Nov. '19 – Aug. '21	21	47%
Sept. '29 – July '32	34	89%
Mar. '37 – Mar. '38	12	49%
Sept '39 – Apr. '42	31	40%
May '46 – June '49	37	23%
Apr. '56 – Oct. '57	18	19%
Jan. '60 – Oct. '60	9	17%
Dec. '61 – June '62	7	27%
Feb. '66 – Oct. '66	8	25%
Dec. '68 – May '70	18	36%
Jan. '73 – Dec. '74	23	45%
Sept. '76 – Feb. '78	17	27%
Apr. '81 – Aug. '82	16	24%
	Average 19 Months	Average 36%

Fig. 1-14. Past Bear Markets (Courtesy of BCA Publications Ltd.)

_____Table 1-2 Election Years_____
Highs and Lows

Month Reached	Number of Times Dow Reached	
	High	Low
January	4	3
February	0	3
March	1	3
April	1	1
May	0	2
June	1	2
July	0	1
August	0	0
September	1	0
October	1	1
November	4	0
December	4	1
Total representing 17 Presidential Election Years	17	17

presidential election years (up to 1988) in which the Dow Industrials was lower at the end of the year than at the beginning.

Glancing at Table 1-2, you will also find that never in the 17 presidential election years has the Dow reached either its high or low for the year during the month of August. In 15 of the 17 years, the lows for the years were reached prior to August. In addition, only one low was reached in October and one in December, while in 10 out of the 17 years, the highs of the Dow were reached in the last four months of the years.

Investors who buy stocks for a pull of several months, will particularly want to consider the months of July, August, September, or October as being a potential timing factor. However, before the investor takes a positive position, another confirming technical analysis signal should exist. In addition, the investor should base his or her selections of *specific* stocks upon *fundamental analysis*. (See chapter 2.)

THE STOCK MARKET IN YEARS FOLLOWING PRESIDENTIAL ELECTION YEARS

During the 18 years following each of the presidential election years, the Dow Industrials reached its highs and lows, as shown in Table 1-3.

_____Table 1-3 Highs and Lows_____
in Years After Election Years

Month Reached	Number of Times Dow reached	
	High	Low
January	4	4
February	0	1
March	1	2
April	1	0
May	1	0
June	0	2
July	2	0
August	0	1
September	1	2
October	1	2
November	1	1
December	6	3
	18	18

You'll note that in the 18 years following each presidential election years, the Dow Industrials never reached a low point in April, May, or July and never reached a high in February, June, or August.

For investors who believe history repeats itself and who are short-term oriented, such data may be of some help. If the Dow Industrials is at a high point, so far in the year, in June or August we know that in the 18 years following the presidential election year, those months were never the year's highest for the Dow. Therefore, if history repeats itself, some subsequent month should be the high for the year.

If the Dow is at the high point for the year during the month of September, based upon past performance the chances are the Dow will hit a higher high for the year in the month of December.

A RALPH GOLDMAN MARKET TURNAROUND SIGNAL

The shares of nearly 2000 companies are traded daily on the N.Y. Composite System. A sample of a week's trading might look like this:

	M	*T*	*W*	*T*	*F*
			NYSE Composite		
Issues traded	1970	1980	1975	1992	1986
Advances	1250	710	680	917	790
Declines	347	800	810	582	740
Unchanged	373	470	485	493	456

Ralph Goldman, a stock broker in Ft. Lauderdale, Florida, believes a record of such trading can point to a possible change in market direction. He maintains that when 500 or more shares are traded that are unchanged in price from the previous closing price on four or more consecutive days, it offers a possible change in the market from up to down or from down to up. Let's explore this view's rationale.

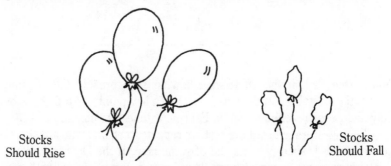

Stocks
Should Rise

Stocks
Should Fall

Fig. 1-15. A Ralph Goldman Turnaround Signal (Sketch by Holly Wilson-Perrotto)

There comes a time in all rising stock markets when prices reach higher and higher peaks. When that happens, more of the normal investors begin to hesitate to pay a still higher price for a stock. Simultaneously, the owners of a stock might be willing to sell at the previous day's closing price but not lower, believing the bull market still has a way to go. So, a larger number of shares are traded unchanged in price. When that happens to 500 or more for four or more consecutive days, it suggests a possible turnaround in the market, from up to down.

The opposite would seem to prevail nearing a market bottom. Those who have held all their stocks during a long downhill in the market reason that they have held their stocks this long and refuse to sell them at a still lower price. At the same time, those who buy do not want to pay a price any higher than the previous close, thinking it might go still lower. Thus, the number of shares traded but unchanged in price increases.

While I know of no precise results of this signal having been recorded, it is known to have been correct on some occasions.

SHORT SALES OF SPECIALISTS VS. THE PUBLIC'S

All investors recognize that when the market is reaching a high point, most individuals are buying stocks and few are selling. When this occurs, and the buy orders cannot be met by the public's or member's sell orders, the function of the specialist is triggered. If the specialist cannot meet the unfilled buy orders from his personal inventory in his investment account, he must sell short in his trading account.

It is often beneficial for a trader to observe the relationship of specialists' vs. the public's short sales. During the week of August 28, 1987 the Dow Industrials reached its all-time high of 2740. Two weeks earlier it seemed almost a telltale signal that a drop in the market was imminent when the specialists' short sales more than doubled those of the public.

Week of 8/14/87	Short Sales
By the Public	28,070,000
By Specialists	56,463,000

During the next two months the Dow Industrials dropped 1120 points to an intraday low of 1620 on October 19, 1987.

Even during periods of a narrow trading range, it may be advisable for traders to observe the switch in the specialists' short sales relative to the public's short sales.

On a number of occasions it seemed almost uncanny for a market gain to soon occur after the short sales of the public became higher than those of the specialists, as shown below:

	Short Sales		Dow		
Week of	Specialists	Public	Average	Date	Point Gain
5/13/88	15,375,000	18,954,000	1956.44	5/27/88	
			2152.28	6/22/88	195.84
8/12/88	16,230,000	19,841,000	1989.30	8/13/88	
			2112.91	9/30/88	123.61
10/28/88	19,504,000	20,037,000	2054.03	11/11/88	
			2358.93	2/ 8/89	304.90

	Short Sales		Dow		
Week of	Specialists	Public	Average	Date	Point Gain
2/9/90	25,554,000	29,155,000	2564.19	2/23/90	
			2765.77	4/17/90	201.58
4/20/90	19,987,400	22,258,400	2645.05	4/30/90	
			2999.75	7/16/90	354.70

MOVING AVERAGE LINES

A number of well-known stock market advisers concentrate on analysis of moving averages. When they find the trend of the market to be negative by referring, for example, to signals such as the 30-day moving average of the Dow Industrials or the S&P 500, they recommend lightening up on stocks in general. With respect to a particular stock, when its current price falls below its own 30-day moving average, some analysts recommend selling the stock.

Fig. 1-16. Moving Average Line Can Indicate a Change in Direction of the Market or of a Specific Stock

A 30-day moving average is simple to maintain once it is constructed. It is formulated by adding the closing price of the stock, Dow, or S&P 500 for 30 days and dividing the total by 30. Each day thereafter, the 30-day old figure should be subtracted, the current day's figure should be added, and the new total should be divided by 30. When the trend moves above or below the average, it is considered bullish or bearish, respectively.

Maintaining moving averages for a large number of stocks can be time-consuming, and significant changes do not occur very frequently. For example, after changing directions, the Dow Industrials moved up or down 100 points or more only 30 times in 20 years, an average of $1^1/_2$ times a year.

A FEW ROBERT STOVALL INDICATORS

Robert Stovall, head of Stovall Twenty-First Advisors, originated several "event" indicators. I'm including several here for interest's sake.

While such indicators are not supported by any fundamental or technical factors, the results have most often proven correct.

The Triple Crown Winners

In the long history of the Triple Crown, there have been only eleven occasions when the same horse won all three races. The Kentucky Derby, the Preakness, and the Belmont Stakes. In eight of these eleven years, the stock market dropped.

The Super Bowl Winners

Each year, millions of Americans anxiously anticipate the Super Bowl football game. In 1978, Robert Stovall recognized a strong correlation between the conference team winning the Super Bowl game and the stock market. This signal holds that when an original NFL team wins the game, the stock market will have an up-year. If a former AFL team wins, the stock market will be lower at the end of the year than at the beginning. So far, the predictor has been correct about the stock market in 21 of 23 years.

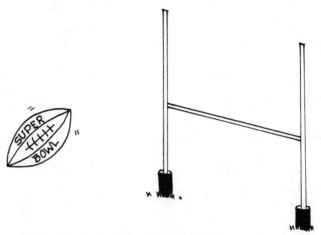

Fig. 1-17. The Super-Bowl Winners—A Robert Stovall Indicator of Up and Down Market Years (Sketch by Holly Wilson-Perrotto)

Robert Stovall's Bellwether Theory—A Bull or Bear Market Indicator

The Bellwether Theory maintains that in the event the market price of General Motors stock does not fall below a previous low point within a three-month period, it heralds an upward move in the stock market. Also, if General Motors stock does not make a higher high within three months, a market downtrend is signalled.

The Hemline Indicator

From time to time with the changes in fashion it has been noted that when the hemline of women's garments is shortened, the stock market rises, and when lengthened, the market drops. While this indicator lacks any economic foundation, the gurus of Wall Street believe it worthy enough to bring it to the attention of the investing public each time it occurs. (However, these days with the "anything goes" attitude toward hemlines, this indicator would be nearly impossible to plot.)

- Originator of Indicator: Unknown.
- Results of Indicator: Unknown.

Rising
Hemline
--
Rising
Market

Falling
Hemline
--
Falling
Market

Fig. 1-18. The Hemline Indicator Predicts Rising or Falling Markets (Sketch by Holly Wilson-Perrotto)

NUMBER OF SHARES IN SPECIALISTS' INVENTORIES—A Possible Technical Analysis Signal

When an investor gives his broker an order to buy (or sell) a stock, it is routed to the firm's floor broker at the appropriate stock exchange. The floor broker proceeds to the area of the post of the specialist, who is responsible for trading in that stock.

With a public outcry, your floor broker calls for current quotes on the stock of your order. The specialist, who maintains a book "away from the market orders," quotes the best bid and ask prices. If no other floor broker accepts the trade offered by your broker, the specialist steps in and accepts your order for his personal account.

While the rules governing the activities of the specialists vary somewhat by different exchanges, on the New York Stock Exchange, the specialists maintain two accounts to cover their personal transactions. One is an "investment account," for which the specialist can buy and sell stocks. The other is a "trading account," for which he can buy or sell stocks and also execute "short sales." He is not permitted to sell stock short from his investment account.

When the specialist fills a buy order he can do so by selling from his inventory of the stock in either his investment or trading accounts, or if he so chooses, he may sell the stock short in his trading account to match the customer's buy order.

The opposite occurs when the investor's order is to sell a stock. If it reaches the specialist for consummation, he will buy the stock for either his investment or trading account.

So we find that when the pendulum of public perception swings to an extreme and there are no public orders to buy, the specialist buys for his personal accounts to meet the sell orders. When there are no public orders to sell, he sells from either of his accounts or sells short to meet the buy orders. In other words, the specialist is not permitted to initiate transactions, only to accommodate them.

The priority of consideration given to the public's orders by the stock exchanges with specialists does not apply when buying or selling stocks in the "over-the-counter" market. On NASDAQ the customer orders are not required to take precedence over the market-makers in the stock. They can execute trades at a bid or ask price for their own accounts before exercising a trade at that price for an outside customer. Furthermore, the spreads between bid and ask prices of stocks on the exchanges are smaller than those traded over-the-counter.

Considering the requirements of the specialist, doesn't it tell us that at the top of the markets, when everyone is buying, the specialist's trading account must contain an abundance of short sales? Contrawise, when the market is at or near a low point, wouldn't the inventories in investment or trading account or both be overloaded? Then, when the market moves in the other direction, the specialist initially is able to recoup some temporary losses and later make profits. After all, the specialist invests risk capital to take positions opposite to the originators of the orders, and he *is* in business to make a profit. The specialist has survived over the years, albeit with setbacks.

Now then, how can the technical analyst make use of this knowledge? It is difficult because, so far as is known, there is no public information as to the size of the specialists' inventories. Furthermore, even if the precise data were available, would it be helpful? For instance, if the specialists had very large inventories, you could assume the public was always wrong in selling extensively. At the opposite extreme, if their inventories were practically nil, you could assume that the public was always wrong in buying with ebullience. However, the public is not always wrong. But since we know the specialists are a durable lot and generally make money over long periods of time, the inventory data *could* be helpful.

Because published information does not include an accounting for inventories in the two accounts of the specialists, the best you can do is to start building a consolidated inventory of the specialists' positions from information that is published in the financial press. To do this, you add their purchases to those of the previous week, and deduct their sales (including short sales) from the purchases.

When the inventories grow to a seemingly large figure and at least two other bullish technical analysis signals are flashing, the market may be near a low point and the purchase of stocks may be warranted. At this time, the investor should be able to buy stocks at prices somewhat lower than what was paid by the specialists.

When the opposite occurs and specialists have little or no inventories and there are two or more bearish technical signals, the time could be ripe for lightening up on stocks.

Finally, it seems fair to mention that criticism has often been levelled at the specialists and seldom have they been lauded for the parts they play in helping to stabilize the markets. When specialists buy stocks at the time a majority of the public is selling, and when they sell stocks when the majority is buying, they are exercising their responsibility in helping to maintain orderly markets.

The extent to which specialists participate in the overall trading activity on the American Stock Exchange, for example, is depicted in Fig. 1-19.[1]

The foregoing specialist participation has proven to be extremely effective in stabilizing the market by moderating volatility. Figure 1-20 shows that the specialists of the American Stock Exchange have been able to lessen the volatility of the market by a rate of 96.3% by their participation.

There has been much publicity of late concerning the development of a 100% computerized trading system for the stock exchanges.

---

[1]Figures 1-19 and 1-20 are adapted with permission from American Stock Exchange Pamphlet "Quality of Markets Report."

**Specialist Participation
as a Percentage of Volume, 1983**

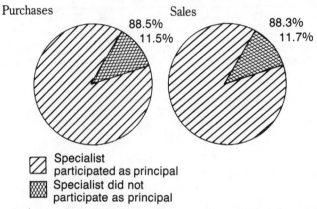

Purchases

Sales

88.5%
11.5%

88.3%
11.7%

⬜ Specialist
   participated as principal
▨ Specialist did not
   participate as principal

Fig. 1-19. Specialists Participation (Courtesy of American Stock Exchange)

Under such a system all buy and sell orders would be entered into the system for matching and execution. If this occurs, the functions of the specialists would, per se, be eliminated.

Many specialists would still most likely be buyers and sellers of stocks, but on a much lower-volume basis since they would then have to pay commissions, the same as everyone else.

Without the effect of the stabilizing activity of the present specialists when a fully computerized system is adopted, it is difficult to estimate the degree of volatility of the then market. It seems probable that the market will be affected by greater volatility and more severe swings both up and down. Of course, circuit breakers will be applied that will stop all computer input for specified periods of time. Only the future will tell whether such artificial restraints will prove to exacerbate rather than quell volatility.

**Specialist
Stabilization Rate, 1983**

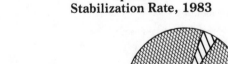

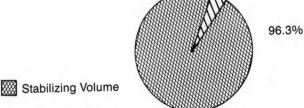

96.3%

▨ Stabilizing Volume

Fig. 1-20. Specialists Stabilization Rate (Courtesy of American Stock Exchange)

USING TECHNICAL ANALYSIS

Making use of technical analysis signals may offer the investor the most likely opportunity to identify the "timing" of when to enter or exit the stock market. The technical signals furnished in these pages have been assigned a subjective value rating (on a scale of 1 to 10), as shown in Table 1-4. A similar rating for fundamental factors follows the examination of fundamental analysis in chapter 2.

As you study the table, please consider the following:

1. In the merit rating scale of 1 to 10, there are four signals rated "5." While some of the "5" ratings have had uncanny records, they all are not rated higher because there are no economic, technical, or fundamental bases in support of their predications. Earlier, it was stated that a single technical signal may foretell a switch in market direction. It is advisable not to take action only on the basis of any signal rated "5." One or

Table 1-4 Technical Signals

Technical Signal	Value Rating	Page in Text
Combination of Discount Rate Turnaround and The Dow Theory Signal	10	5
Correlation Between Price Trends and Volume Signal	10	9
Short Sales of Specialists vs. The Publics	10	27
Number of Shares in Specialists' Inventories	10	30
Contrary Opinion Sentiment Indicator— The Put-Call Ratio	9	20
Insider Sell-Buy Ratio	9	21
The Stock Market in Presidential Election Years	9	22
The Stock Market in Years Following Presidential Election Years	9	24
Head and Shoulders Formations	9	8
A Ralph Goldman Turnaround Signal	8	26
Advance-Decline Lines	8	8
Moving Average Line Indicator	7	28
Will the October 1987 Crash Follow the Pattern of the October 1929 Debacle	6	22
The Hemline Indicator	5	30
The Triple Crown Indicator	5	29
Robert Stovall's Bell Weather Theory	5	28
The Super-Bowl Indicator	5	29

more of such signals should also coincide with one or more signals rated 6 through 10.

2. Any technical signal rated lower than 5 is not considered meritorious enough for listing here.

3. The relative ratings given to the different technical signals are purely subjective, based upon empirical recognition of these market influences, and are not extrapolated from statistical data. If and when you apply these factors to future market action, you may want to change the value ratings to your liking. Regardless of the different ratings, all deserve consideration in deciding when to buy or sell stocks.

There is little doubt as to the value of technical analysis. However, technical analysis signals alone are akin to a half-filled balloon. Fundamental analysis is also a necessary ingredient of a sound investment policy.

TECHNICAL ANALYSIS ALONE IS NOT ENOUGH

The foregoing pages reflect the importance of making use of technical analysis in assessing possible changes in stock market trends, and entrance and exit points. Over a period of time, an investor should not always expect to be successful in the stock market by buying stocks based only upon technical analysis timing. A list of highs and lows on a given day 20 years ago and a similar list 20 years later are shown in Fig. 1-21.

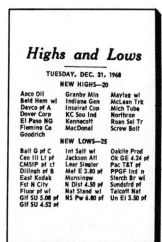

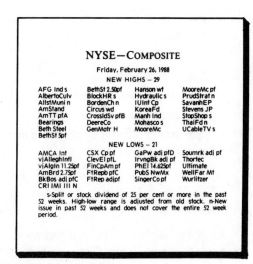

Fig. 1-21. Highs and Lows of Stocks

Individuals who had previously bought and held stocks on the new low lists had paper losses. Those who had bought and held stocks on the new high lists had paper profits. Is any more striking evidence needed to make sound selections when buying stocks?

This brings us to a presentation of fundamental analysis.

SOME TECHNICAL FACTORS
LOSE THEIR SIGNIFICANCE

Remember the words of Socrates who, when contemplating the serious problems of the day, said: "Even this shall come to pass."

Throughout our economic history many factors have been viewed as magnified matters of the moment. There was a time when thousands in the financial world eagerly waited for the market-closing each Thursday so they would be among the first to learn the new MI figures. Later, matters concerning the discount rate, the prime rate, the federal funds rate, the import-export imbalance, and the federal budget deficit, among others, have loomed large. Often, attention shifted from one to another with a new leader of importance moving to the forefront; much like the changing leaders of a V-shaped flock of geese migrating with the change of seasons. Nonetheless, some have stood out (and some still do), shining in the bright lights of the Stock Market Marquee.

* * *

An investor's chances of making a prudent move in the stock market improve when:

- Several technical signals concurrently change from flashing red to green.
- The market has sustained a significant drop and appears to be close to a bottom.
- Gloom is widespread and pessimism prevails.
- The "bears" are dancing about in glee.
- A pall overhangs the boardrooms in brokers' offices throughout America.
- "Money" takes on added importance.
- The Budget Deficit appears hopeless and the politicians helpless.

All of the above seems well and good, but the question remains about *which* stocks to buy. This is where fundamental analysis comes in.

The primary objective of fundamental analysis is to preidentify stocks suitable for potential purchase. Then, when the timing for investing seems right, based upon technical analysis, most of the fundamental analysis has already been accomplished and the investor won't have to look around excitedly for stocks to buy. All that remains is to relate the intrinsic value of a company's stock to the then current market price.

In the next chapter, we will carefully examine fundamental analysis and its uses.

Fundamental Analysis and Stock Market Strategy

FUNDAMENTAL ANALYSIS INVOLVES SEARCHING OUT FACTS AND influences that affect the operating results of a company and probing into its financial structure in order to assess its intrinsic value.

SOURCE MATERIAL

One of the best sources for obtaining information about a company is to visit the company and have a one-on-one meeting with one of the officers. Other excellent sources are the annual reports of companies. An in-depth analysis of those reports can reveal a wealth of information. (*Note:* In the months of April and May, *Barron's* publishes lists of hundreds of companies whose annual reports are available for free by returning a form with a box checked off for each report requested.)

When examining a company's annual report, be sure to concentrate on the following features:

1. *The footnotes to the financial statements.* These often reveal important details that have a potential impact on the financial affairs of the company. The footnotes could include such information as impending law suits, contingent liabilities, and so forth.

2. *The letter to the stockholders.* Of course, the chairman and president usually put forth the company's best face possible. Still, the letter may allude to the capability of its management, and management is a key to the future of a company.

3. *The balance sheet and the profit and loss statement.* These should be carefully reviewed to see what makes them tick. The interrelated elements of the balance sheet and the profit and loss statement should be compared to analyze the company's results and its financial viability.

The Balance Sheet

A company's balance sheet reflects the dollar value of each of its assets (left side) and each of its liabilities, plus its capital stock and surplus (right side). The total dollar amount of each side is equal.

A balance sheet is usually published at the end of each quarter and at the end of a calendar or fiscal year. Consider it as a snapshot of the dollar amounts given to each component at a given moment. The very next business day, the values will change. Yet, by comparing the figures by quarter with the previous quarter or previous year's quarter, or comparing the end of the year figures with the previous year's figures, you can discover many positive or negative fundamental factors about the company.

After analyzing such fundamental factors with respect to a balance sheet and a profit and loss statement (presented later), you can peg a stock for potential purchase. (See Fig. 2-1.)

WORKING CAPITAL RATIO

Working capital represents the excess of current assets over current liabilities. When the ratio of current assets to current liabilities is 2:1 or over, it is a "plus factor" in fundamental analysis.

Current Assets

Current assets represent cash or cash equivalents and assets that are converted into cash, usually within three or four months.

Current Liabilities

Current liabilities are those that are usually payable within one year, such as accrued taxes, accrued wages, accounts payable, and short term notes payable.

Note in Fig. 2-2 that the ratio of current assets to current liabilities of XYZ Company is almost 4:1. The usual acceptable ratio is 2:1.

XYZ Company

Balance Sheet – December 31, 1988

Assets

Current Assets:

Cash		$1,900,000
Accounts receivable	$5,100,000	
Less reserve for bad debts	– 100,000	5,000,000
Inventory		5,000,000
Total current assets		$11,900,000
Deferred charges		47,000
Fixed assets	$6,800,000	
Less reserve for depreciation	–2,300,000	4,500,000
Excess of cost over value of net assets acquired		1,296,300
Total Assets		$17,743,300

Liabilities and Equity

Current Liabilities:

Accounts payable		$ 1,000,000
Notes payable		1,500,000
Accrued wages		200,000
Accrued taxes		1,300,000
Total Current Liabilities		$ 4,000,000
Long-term Debt		1,000,000
Capital Stock and Equity:		
Capital stock authorized 10,000,000 shares $.01 par value; issued and outstanding 2,330,000		23,300
Paid-in capital		9,820,000
Earned surplus:		
Balance – 1/1/88	$1,500,000	
Net profit for year	+1,400,000	
Balance – 12/31/88		2,900,000
Total Liabilities and Equity		$17,743,300

Fig. 2-1. Balance Sheet

$11.9M	$4.0M
Current Assets	*Current Liabilities*
Cash	Accounts Payable
Accounts Receivable	Notes Payable
Inventories	Accrued Wages
	Accrued Taxes

Fig. 2-2. Working Capital Ratio

A higher ratio may indicate excessive cash on hand that could be put to more productive use.

"AGEING" OF ACCOUNTS RECEIVABLE—
A Potential Negative Factor

After a company's product is financed, manufactured, warehoused, sold, and delivered to a customer, the dollar amount of the sale is not generally paid for in cash. Thus, during each business cycle a part of the sum total of corporate effort temporarily reposes in its accounts receivable.

A normal time span for the collection of accounts receivable runs from 10 to 60 days. When accounts are uncollected for more than 60 to 90 days, they are considered past due.

If management instills in its employees the importance of prompt and courteous treatment of its customers, it should expect reasonably prompt payment of its invoices. Unfortunately, that is not always the case. If the uncollected amount is large enough, it could become a problem for the company. That is why when an independent C.P.A. audits the books of a company, he makes a check of the age of the accounts receivable to be sure that the profit and loss statement contains a sufficient expense charge for bad debts and that the reserve for bad debts is adequate.

The above situation recalls a case in which an accountant of a C.P.A. firm was auditing the books of one of America's most prestigeous residential hotels located on Fifth Avenue, New York City. In the course of "ageing" the hotel's accounts receivable, the accountant found an account with a past-due balance of over $30,000. When he approached the treasurer of the hotel about the account, he was told an almost unbelievable story. The indebted resident was an elderly woman (name deliberately withheld) who was the mother of a famous multimillionaire. The son was also the head of a Fortune 500 Company.

The woman might well have been at least a bit eccentric. She had an 11-room apartment at the hotel and also had six or seven dogs. She previously had the hotel's carpenter cut large holes out of the bottom of walls of connecting rooms so the dogs could have free access throughout the place. When it came to feeding time, the woman called room service to bring meals for the dogs, ordering from the hotel restaurant's menu. The dogs were walked in Central Park by one of the hotel's bellhops.

The woman's son allowed her a $5,000 a month living allowance, much of which went to the hotel. The hotel did not choose to press the lady for payment because of her stature, the family name, and the belief that, if necessary, the son would pay the tab.

In our more modern times an investor does not have an opportunity to have access to the detailed accounts receivable files of a company. There is, however, a method of gauging a company's effectiveness in collecting its accounts receivable. For most going concerns, a test of the collection process can be accomplished as follows:

1. Divide the dollar amount of sales of the year by 12 to obtain the "average monthly sales."

2. If the amount of the accounts receivable on date of the balance sheet exceeds three times the monthly average of sales, it means that some of the accounts receivable are probably more than two months old, which exceeds the normal 60-day collection time span.

3. To see if the collection process is improving or deteriorating, an investor can refer to comparative profit and loss statements and balance sheets covering two-year periods, and repeat the calculations in steps 1 and 2.

If the collection process is deteriorating, a question arises whether the reserve for bad debts is large enough to cover a substantial loss. In the final analysis many large companies have gone into bankruptcy proceedings, and their creditors have suffered losses which, if large enough, could affect the market price of the creditor's stock.

A potential problem of a company could be magnified if a major portion of its sales are with a single customer. There have been instances, however, where capable management has taken corrective action, resulting in a turnaround in a company's fortunes. Let us review the history of Kellwood Company.

In 1971 Kellwood's stock sold at 43³/₄. In 1981, when 70% of its sales were to Sears Roebuck, its stock sold at $10 a share. Management, however, was knowledgeable enough to know this situation should not long endure. Kellwood Company began to diversify by buying up relatively small companies whose sales were generally under 100 million dollars. (*Note:* Investors can often find this kind of information in the letters to stockholders contained in the Quarterly and Annual Reports of companies.)

The acquisitions of Kellwood gradually broadened its customer base. In 1987 its sales to Sears were lowered to about 40%, and the market price of its stock had rebounded to 28⁷/₈—and that was after two stock splits of 2 for 1 and 3 for 2.

So, here we have a situation when, at a given moment in time, a stock purchase would have been a poor one and a subsequent one would have proved lucrative. This underscores the importance of competent management.

FIXED ASSETS

Fixed assets comprise land, buildings, machinery and equipment, vehicles, furniture and fixtures, and other assets that are estimated to be useful for over one year. All of these assets (except land) are depreciated over their normal useful lives, with a portion of the cost being charged as a "depreciation" expense each year. When the bookkeeping entry is made for the depreciation expense, a similar amount is credited to a *reserve for depreciation account*. Note that these charges for depreciation do not represent cash outlays at the time the charge is made.

EXCESS OF COST OVER VALUE OF NET ASSETS—
Potentially a Negative Factor

When a corporation buys another company, it usually pays more to the selling company than its net asset value. The difference between the net asset value of a company and the amount paid was formerly referred to as *goodwill*. That name seemed to have more of a financial stigma attached to it than its new and fancier name: *excess of cost over value of net assets acquired*. (For our purpose here, we will continue to use the less cumbersome term.)

Although goodwill is carried on the balance sheet as an asset, it generally has little, if any, intrinsic value. The practice of most companies is to write off (*amortize*) goodwill as an expense over a period of

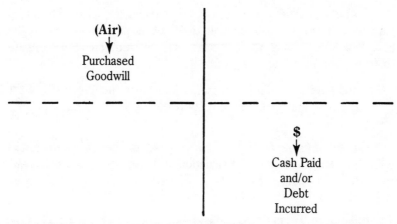

Fig. 2-3. Excess of Cost over Value of Net Assets Acquired can be a Negative Factor

years, but it is not an allowable tax deduction by the I.R.S. for corporate income tax purposes.

DEBT: (FIXED LIABILITIES) TO EQUITY RATIO—
A Plus or Negative Factor

For the debt to equity ratio of companies in manufacturing and service industries (except public utilities) to be considered a plus factor, the dollar amount of equity to the dollar amount of debt must be at least 2 to 1. If the ratio is less than 2 to 1, it should be considered a negative factor. When the ratio is, say, 1 to 5 or 1 to 6 or more, the company is flying by the seat of its pants. (See Fig. 2-4.)

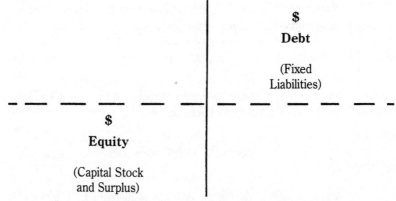

Fig. 2-4. Debt to Equity Ratio: A Plus or Negative Factor

For public utilities, the ratio can be much higher, inasmuch as reg-
ulatory authorities usually permit the debt as part of its asset base
upon which percentage rates of profits are allowed. This helps ensure
that they are operating at a profit.

Fixed liabilities   This represents long-term indebtedness of the
company, which normally matures beyond one year after the balance
sheet date.

Capital stock and equity   This represents the *net worth* of the
company. It is the sum of the valuation of the outstanding stock, paid-
in capital, and retained earnings, as carried on the books of the company.

Capital stock   This consists of the number of shares of stock
authorized, the number outstanding, its par value per share, and treasury stock, if any. Treasury stock is stock that was outstanding but
was then repurchased by the company. Treasury stock can again be
sold or used for any other corporate purpose, including availability for
issuance to employees under stock option plans.

Paid-in capital   This represents the difference between the sum
received for the issuance of stock and its par value.
Paid-in capital is usually associated with the issuance of common
stock that has a very low par value. An example is the XYZ Company
whose common stock carries a par value of 1 cent per share. (Chapter
3 contains a presentation of how *big* money has been made, and can
be made, with low par value per share and paid-in capital being significant factors.)

Earned surplus   This is that portion of a company's equity representing its accumulated earnings after the payment of any dividends.

* * *

Now let's focus upon evaluative factors embodied in the profit and loss
statement of the XYZ Company. (See Fig. 2-5.)

Net sales   Net sales represent gross sales minus returned sales
and allowances.

Cost of goods sold   Cost of goods sold is derived by adding the
amount of net purchases during the year to the amount of the inven-

XYZ Company
Profit and Loss Statement
for the Year Ending December 31, 1988

Net Sales	$20,000,000
Cost of Goods Sold	14,700,000
Gross Profit	$ 5,300,000
Selling and General Administrative Expenses	2,100,000
Depreciation	500,000
	$ 2,700,000
Provision of Taxes	1,300,000
Net Profit	$ 1,400,000

Fig. 2-5. Profit and Loss Statement

tory at the beginning of the year, and then subtracting the amount of the inventory at the end of the year as shown below:

Inventory – January 1		$ 3,500,000
Add purchases	$16,300,000	
Less returns	100,000	16,200,000
		$19,700,000
Less Inventory – December 31		5,000,000
Cost of Goods Sold		$14,700,000

In companies engaged in manufacturing, the inventories at both the beginning and end of the year consist of raw materials, work in process, and finished goods. These inventories are required (by the IRS) to be priced on a consistent basis from year to year, using one of the following methods: the first-in/first-out, the last-in/first-out, or the average cost method. Let's examine these methods further with an example.

Assume cocoa beans are a raw material used in processing. Quantities of a supply of the beans are purchased periodically:

1. *June 1*—Five metric tons are purchased at $1,200 per ton.

2. *Sept. 5*—Twelve metric tons are purchased at $1,150 per ton.

3. *Nov. 10*—Three metric tons are purchased at $1,300 per ton.

Upon receipt the beans are placed in storage. As they are requisitioned from stock the cost of the material is charged to goods in process under the:

- *First-in/first-out method* (see 1. on p. 47) at $1,200 a ton until all five such metric tons are used. Thereafter the twelve tons in 2. above and the three tons in 3. above will be charged out in sequential order at $1,150 a ton and $1,300 a ton, respectively.

- *Last-in/first-out method* (see 3. on p. 47) at $1,300 a ton until all three such metric tons are used. Thereafter the twelve tons in 2. above and the five tons in 1. above will be charged out in that order at $1,150 and $1,200, respectively.

- *Average cost method,* which is calculated as follows:

5	tons at $1,200 equals	$ 6,000
12	tons at $1,150 equals	13,800
3	tons at $1,300 equals	3,900
20		$23,700
	Average cost per ton	$ 1,185

Each ton is thus charged out to goods in process at $1,185 per ton until all raw beans are consumed.

Under all three methods of pricing raw material out to goods in process, their cost ultimately becomes part of cost of goods sold.

FACTORS AFFECTING NET PROFITS

If one were to say, "The XYZ Company earned a profit of $1,400,000 last year," some might believe the company is $1,400,000 richer in cash than it was the year before. This misconception can best be dispelled by comparing the profit and loss statement and the balance sheet.

The last line on a profit and loss statement shows the amount of net profit earned. The net profit is the amount left after deducting all costs and expenses from all income during the period (quarterly or annually). The net profit is added to the amount that was in the earned surplus account at the beginning of the period, and the total (minus dividends paid, if any) is shown on the balance sheet. Note that the XYZ Company's net profit is $1,400,000 shown on the profit and loss statement corresponds with the same amount in the capital stock and equity portion of the balance sheet.

Inasmuch as the $1,400,000 of profits are a part of the earned surplus, the equivalent of these monies are included in a distribution amongst the assets. As an example, when a sale is made, the amount is generally reflected in an increase in the amount of accounts receivable from the customer. As of the balance sheet date, the receivable may not as yet have been paid in cash by the customer. Thus we see that some profits, as of the balance sheet date, were earned and not reflected in cash, but rather in an increase in the amount of accounts receivable. The same applies even after the cash is received, and the cash is subsequently expended for other assets.

NET PROFIT PER SHARE BASED UPON AVERAGE NUMBER OF SHARES OUTSTANDING—A Potential Negative Factor

Practically every publicly owned company reports *Net Profit Per Share*, which is derived based upon the *average number of shares outstanding*. It may benefit the investor to recognize the effect of this practice on the amount of reported profit per share.

In the event a substantial number of additional shares were issued, say, late in the fourth quarter of the year, the average number of shares outstanding divided into the amount of net profit produces a higher reported net profit per share than would be the case had the number of shares outstanding at the end of the year been divided into the net profit.

Moreover, if the additional shares were issued for reasons that may have little chance of improving profits in the new year, or over a longer period, the use of the average number of shares outstanding in computing the net profit per share could be misleading, and therefore would be a Negative Factor (Fig. 2-6).

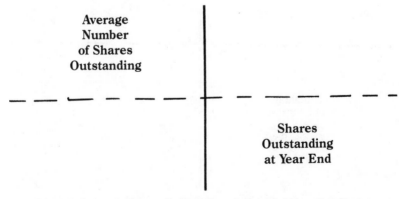

Fig. 2-6. Average Shares Outstanding: A Potential Negative Factor

Two such instances would be:

1. When shares of stock are issued for exercise of options by insiders or employees and the cost to them is less than the book value per share.

2. When a purchase or takeover of a company is made and the value of the shares issued exceeds the net asset value of the selling company. It should be noted that when a portion of the goodwill thus established is written off as an expense each year, it is not allowed by the Internal Revenue Service. So, the amount of goodwill represents an intangible constituting an expense against future operations of the company.

SALES DECREASE VS. COST OF GOODS SOLD DECREASE—A Possible Plus Factor

There are instances where the percentage decrease in the cost of goods sold is greater than the percentage decrease in sales. This results in a higher percentage of gross profit on fewer dollars of sales. While this situation might not be as dramatic as when gross profits increase while sales volume increases, when it happens to a company like General Motors, the investor should sit back and take notice (Fig. 2-7).

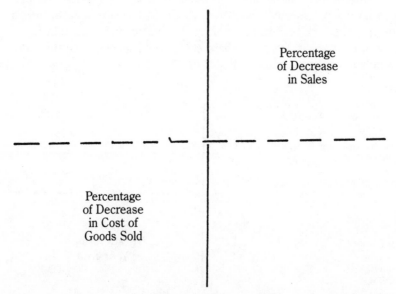

Fig. 2-7. Sales Decrease and Cost of Sales Decrease: A Possible Plus Factor

The following has been extracted from General Motors Corporation 1987 Annual Report:

	1987	1986	Percent Decrease
Net Sales of Manufactured Products	$100,118.5 Mil.	$101,506.9 Mil.	1.38
Cost of Sales and Other Operating Charges	$ 87,204.4 Mil.	$ 89,198.3 Mil.	2.21

Cost Reduction Programs Take Effect. Together with increased product introductions and improved product quality, cost reductions are a cornerstone of the Corporations strategic program to increase earnings. G.M. made significant progress in 1987 toward its goal of achieving permanent cost reductions totalling $10 billion annually by year-end 1990. Major areas of targeted savings include: salaried headcount reductions, $2 billion; reduced staff expense, $200 million; divestitures, restructurings and joint ventures, $200 million; plant closings, $500 million; lower vertical integration, $500,000; and productivity related savings, $6.6 billion.

Cost reductions totaling $3.7 billion were implemented during 1987, the first year of the program. Additional savings of nearly $4 billion are anticipated in 1988. . . .

While the above seems extremely favorable for General Motors over the next few years (barring a poor economic environment), a potential investor should not immediately rush out to buy *any* stock. As you should already know, the timing of stock purchases based upon technical analysis should also be considered.

Since the above paragraphs were written, some time has elapsed and the General Motors Corporation report for the third quarter of 1988 has been received. The following is quoted from it.

And let me reiterate our commitment to enhance stockholder value by achieving a return on common stockholder equity of at least 15% by 1990. The driving force that will move us toward that target is our continuing effort to reduce costs. We're gaining new efficiencies and making productivity improvements. We anticipate additional material savings. And our personal reductions are progressing ahead of schedule. For these and other reasons, our original $10 billion, four-year, cost savings Action Plan is proceeding better than expected. As a result, we have increased our goal of cumulative cost reductions by 1990 to between $12.5 billion and $13 billion.

The larger percentage decrease in cost of goods sold as compared with the percentage decrease in sales of General Motors Corporation could be viewed as a solid Plus Factor. This, combined with information regarding their cost reduction success, adds a second Plus Factor for possible stock purchase. Such a move would have proven successful because of the ensuing rise in the price of the stock and a subsequent 2 for 1 stock split.

MERCHANDISE TURNOVER—
A Comparative Functional Analysis Factor

Throughout corporate America most companies make a profit from the sale of its products. Occasionally there are instances when the more products a company sells, the greater are its losses (see p. 57). The comments given here do not apply to such instances.

When companies sell their products at a profit (with other things being equal), chances are the more they sell the greater will be their profits. In analysing results, a factor that comes into play is: how many times a company's products are moved by sale (merchandise turnover) as compared to their competitive companies (Fig. 2-8).

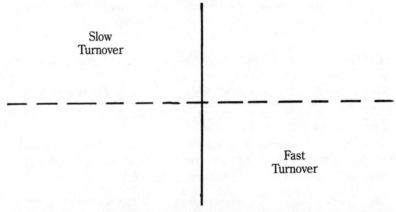

Slow
Turnover

Fast
Turnover

Fig. 2-8. Merchandise Turnover—A Comparative Functional Analysis Factor

Very rarely are specific figures published with respect to merchandise turnover. There is, however, a way to make a comparative analysis between competing companies. Many companies disclose the dollar amounts of their inventories for two successive years under the current assets caption on their balance sheets and the cost of goods sold figures on their profit and loss statements contained in their annual reports. Also *Moody's Industrial Manual* publishes detailed financial data by company, covering 5 to 7 consecutive years and including the dollar amounts of inventories and cost of goods sold.

To find an approximate comparative merchandise turnover rate by companies:

1. Add the year-ending amounts of merchandise inventory for two successive years and divide by two.
2. Divide the amount derived in step 1 into the latest year's cost of goods sold amount to arrive at the approximate merchandise turnover rate.

A comparison can then be made of competing companies that make a profit. With other things equal, the higher the turnover rate, the more positive the factor.

STOCK PRICES REACT TO EARNINGS

There is little doubt that stock prices often react to news of decreases or increases in earnings of corporations. To illustrate this point, let's look at a few headlines from the *Wall Street Journal*.

Headline: "Advance Micro Devices Reports 1986 1st Quarter Deficit of 49 Cents."
The stock then proceeded to drop 18 points in the next nine months (from 32 to 14).

Headline: "IBM's Profit $2.40 per Share."
The stock dropped nearly 3 points the next day. Why? Because *"the Street* expected somewhat higher earnings."

Because stock prices are so responsive to earnings, the investor who employs fundamental analysis looks beyond the headlines. Perhaps the blazing notoriety was justified, perhaps not.

COMPARISON OF PROFITS AND SALES WITH PRIOR YEAR OR QUARTER-TO-QUARTER

Another factor to consider in analyzing the value of common stock of a company is the trend of its sales and profits. If both trends are down, there could be many reasons for this, and some might not be public knowledge. It is generally best to look elsewhere for a possible investment. If both sales and earnings are in uptrends, further analysis is usually justified.

To illustrate a point: Let's assume a strictly hypothetical situation by considering the only expenses of a company are depreciation and amortization of goodwill. If there was no increase in fixed assets or goodwill during the year, the write-off expenses in comparative profit and loss statements would remain constant. Let's also assume there was an increase in sales of $1,000,000:

	1988	1987
Net Sales	$6,000,000	$6,000,000
Depreciation	500,000	500,000
Amortization of Goodwill	100,000	100,000
Total Expenses	$ 600,000	$ 600,000
Net Profit	$5,400,000	$4,400,000

As you can see in the above, constant charges for depreciation and amortization are not an additional drag against any profit accruing from an increase in the dollar amount of sales. For this, management might be credited for the improvement in sales. Yet such an increase could have been due strictly to improvement in economic conditions.

Remember the previously made comment that management was a "key to the future of a company"? Some investors make an effort to determine management effectiveness by making an analysis of the incremental net profit of a company compared with its incremental increase in net sales.

ABC Company

	1988	1987
Dec. 31 Quarter:		
Total Sales	$7,101,672	$5,726,722
Net Income	929,452	414,968
Sept. 30 Quarter:		
Total Sales	6,557,488	5,576,480
Net Income	786,431	385,013

Even though depreciation and amortization account for part of the incremental net income, it is possible some betterment has occurred in conducting the affairs of the company. So, on the face of it, it looks like the stock of the ABC Company may be considered for purchase. Right? Well, maybe. First, the fundamental analyst should examine whether improvement in profits are more closely associated with the effort of management. The analyst may refer to the incremental gross profit on sales, rather than on net profits, in order to eliminate any effect of depreciation or amortization on the profit picture.

	1988	%	1987	%	Incremental Increase	
					Amount	%
Net Sales	$120,000	100	$100,000	100	$20,000	20
Cost of Goods Sold	65,000	54.1	50,000	50	15,000	30
Gross Profit on Sales	$ 55,000	45.9	$ 50,000	50	$ 5,000	10%

The above gross profit on sales represents an incremental increase of 10% for 1988 compared with 1987, and any benefit accruing from the depreciation and amortization factors do not apply in this comparison. So, again at first blush, this looks like a favorable situation. But let's examine these figures a little closer. We find that although sales showed an increase of 20%, the gross profit on sales declined percentagewise by .10. That was because the cost of goods sold increased more proportionately than the increase in net sales. A continuation of that trend could transform what appeared to be a positive factor into a negative one.

By referring to many corporate annual reports, we know that the dollar amount of the cost of goods sold is 2 to 10 or more times greater than the total of all other costs and expenses combined. So now, finally, the more knowledgeable fundamental analyst will make a much better comparative analysis, which can point directly to the effectiveness of management by concentrating on a comparison of the incremental increase in the *cost of goods sold* with the incremental increase in *net sales*.

For example:

	1988	%	1987	%	Incremental Increase	
					Amount	%
Net Sales	$120,000	100	$100,000	100	$20,000	20
Cost of Goods Sold	55,000	45.9	50,000	50	5,000	10
Gross Profit on Sales	$ 65,000	50.1	$ 50,000	50	$15,000	30%

When an increase in gross profit on sales is due to a lower percentage increase in cost of goods sold compared with the percentage increase in net sales, it can be the result of improved manufacturing productivity, changes in the assembly process, reduced waste, reduction in factory overhead costs, and reduced costs in unit output—all of which can be directly attributable to management.

There are two rare exceptions to this assessment. The first represents that unusual situation when the purchase cost of raw materials is reduced (and the company uses the last-in, first-out method of costing-out raw materials). The second is when the pricing or volume of the inventories are incorrect. But we should emphasize here that it is almost always through management *changes* that progress is made.

Attempting to convince workers of the benefits to be derived from making changes in their work routines is one of management's toughest problems. The offhand response to a suggested change invariably is: "You can't do that."

Good management knows that improvements do not come about by waving a magic wand, and they also recognize the natural reluctance on the part of workers to change. They know the workers are experienced in their work routines and prefer the status quo, and they also know that within most people lies an ever-present sense of accomplishment—from the old-time craftsman who took pride in carving his "mark" on his finished product, to the floor sweeper in a factory who, when finished, looks around and says, "It looks nice and clean," to the chairman of the board of a major corporation.

The above discussion on reluctance to change brings to mind two stories of management in a long gone era:

At the turn of the century, Charles Kettering became chief engineer at General Motors Corporation. He soon learned of a huge backup in the portion of assembly line where the automobiles were being painted. Kettering asked the foreman, "Why are the cars backed up so long?" The reply: "Because it takes nature three days for the paint to dry."

Sometime later, Kettering noticed a colored ashtray in the window of a curio shop on Fifth Avenue in New York City. Upon inquiry, he learned the trays were made by a woman in the basement of her home in New Jersey. Kettering visited the woman and told her how much he admired her work and asked, "What do you paint them with?" The woman replied, "Lacquer." The woman sold a gallon of the lacquer to Kettering, who took it back to Detroit. He said to the paint foreman: "I want you to try this lacquer in painting the cars." The foreman instantly replied: "You can't use that . . . it dries too fast." Since then, over 100,000,000 cars have been painted with lacquer.

Frederick W. Taylor was the father of scientific management and probably the world's first efficiency expert (now referred to as management consultant). He was aware of the importance of the sense of accomplishment in workers. Soon after he was hired to manage a foundry with carte blanche authority to make any and all changes he saw fit, he learned of unrest brewing amongst the skilled workers. The men believed they should have an increase in wages. They were good workers, but Taylor knew the economics of competition would not permit passing on the increased salary costs to the customers of the company.

When Taylor sensed the workers were about to go on strike, he told them, "I have a new job for you. Follow me." He led them to a yard behind the foundry and said, "See that huge pile of bricks over there? Well, pick them up, take them over to the other end of the yard, and place them down carefully so they don't chip. For this work we will pay you one dollar a day more." When the day was half over, the foreman came to Taylor and said: "The bricks are all moved. What should we do now?" Taylor replied, "Put them back where they were and be sure not to chip any."

The second day the men were told to do the same as on the previous day. On the third day when told to repeat the performance, the foreman steamed, "To hell with that. We'll take our old jobs back and forget the extra dollar a day."

DECREASE IN SALES, INCREASE IN PROFITS

While it might be most advantageous to make a year-to-year or quarter-to-quarter comparison of cost of goods sold (see "Stock Prices React to Earnings" on p. 53), such data are not always readily available. However, it is always possible to make comparisons of net profits to sales. These figures are published daily in financial newspapers.

Occasionally the analyst comes across a situation where sales decrease while profits increase (Fig. 2-9). This is very rare, and it is even more rare that an explanation of such unusual results is made known (except perhaps in the annual report of the company).

A number of years ago the following information was published:

Tokheim Corp.

	Sales	Profit Per Share
Quarter ended May 1976	$19,500,000	.30
Quarter ended May 1977	18,300,000	.43
May Quarter 1977 vs. 1976	−$ 1,200,000	+.13

No explanation of the reasons for the unusual results was offered in the press release. It could have meant that cost savings measures

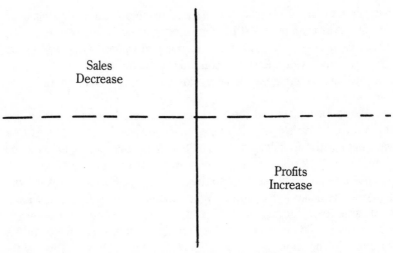

Fig. 2-9. Decrease in Sales—Increase in Profits: A Potentially Strong Positive Factor

had been effected by the company—that it was becoming "lean and mean" and could be in a favorable position of even better profit performance once the trend in sales was reversed.

During the three years following release of the above figures, the high and low market prices of the stock of Tokheim are shown below:

	Market Price Per Share	
	High	*Low*
1977	13¹/₂	9³/₈
1978	19¹/₂	10¹/₄
1979	25⁷/₈	15

A more recent example concerns Nicolet Instrument Corporation. Its revenues decreased and profits increased as shown below:

Nicolet Instrument Corporation

	Sales	*Profits*
Year 1985	126.4 Mil.	.44
Year 1986	121.6 Mil.	.82
	− 4.8 Mil.	+ .38

	Market Price Per Share	
	High	Low
Year 1985	18³/₄	11³/₄
Year 1986	22¹/₈	12³/₈
Year 1987	35¹/₄	18¹/₄

In each of the above cases (Tokheim and Nicolet), another reason profits increased while sales declined could be that fewer shares of stocks were outstanding.

INSIDER ACTIVITY—A Fundamental Analysis Indicator

Individuals, whether John Q. Public or the chairman, director, or officer of a company, may have many reasons for selling stocks, but have only one to buy them: to make a profit.

The following comments do not apply to insiders who make purchases because of some advance knowledge of an impending deal or to arbitraguers or raiders engaged in merger negotiations. The comments made here apply to insider directors and officers who can and do legally purchase stock in their own company.

Every director and officer, as well as outsiders, who already own at least 5% of the common stock of a company must report all subsequent transactions (even as little as 100 shares) to the SEC. Once monthly the SEC publishes the insider transactions, which then become public information.

The stock exchanges also have strict requirements with respect to insider trading. An insider cannot trade in his or her own company's stock based upon inside information that could benefit or hurt the company before such information is made public. This is to ensure that investors can take advantage of the information prior to action taken by the insiders. Furthermore, even when the information is made public, the insider must allow sufficient time to elapse to give the public such opportunity.

Notwithstanding the rigid requirements placed upon insider transactions, there are many instances when insiders can legally purchase stocks in their own company. One, for example, might be that the sum total of all the company's activities point to a possibility of improved earnings. Another might be because of general improvement in their market penetration for new products or improved local or nationwide economic conditions.

At this point you might ask, "Aren't the directors and officers of a company in a favorable position to be aware of all there is to know about its affairs and prospects?" Well, they certainly should be. You might also ask, "Should the investor buy stock in a company at a lower price than was paid for the stock by its very own insiders?" My answer to this last question is "Probably yes." And John Q. Public might benefit by doing so if he does a little research, has patience, and picks the spot at which to buy at lower prices than was paid by the insiders.

During the past 15 years, the Dow Industrials dropped more than 200 points on six occasions. The market price of many stocks dropped substantially, along with the Dow, during these major declines. Often, when the public perception becomes widespread in believing further declines lie ahead and many investors run for the exits, it can set up a subsequent favorable buying opportunity.

A number of financial publications, such as *Value Line Investment Survey*, furnish records of insider purchases and sales, including their names, positions, number of shares purchased or sold, the dates of the transactions, and the prices per share. While the data are usually more than a month old when published, the delay may well prove to be a benefit in disguise.

Such reference material is only one source of information that can be useful following a big drop in the market. When applying one or more technical analysis signals to determine the "timing" of a buying opportunity, the investor could decide to make a stock purchase in a company at a substantially lower price than was paid for the stock by one or more of its officers or directors who, when they bought the stock, thought it was then underpriced.

Such a situation brings exhilaration to the investor; it stimulates feelings of being smart and of acting intelligently. If and when the investment proves lucrative, the investor also experiences a sense of accomplishment.

Table 2-1 furnishes data with respect to the last of the six major declines mentioned above, some prior insider purchases, and the opportunity that was offered the investor, John Q. Public.

COMPANY PURCHASE OF TREASURY STOCK

With respect to the discussion on insider purchases, an investor might well follow the same strategy when it becomes known a company is buying its own stock on the open market for corporate purposes.

Among other things, management believes that the dollars in-

Table 2-1 Insider Activity

Purchases by Directors or Officers of	Purchases—1987			Market Price	
	Number of Shares	When Bought	Price Paid	Subsequent Low	4 Months Later
A.F.G. Industries	20,000	Sept. – Oct.	$31^3/4 – 32^1/8$	21	$32^1/8$
Great A. & P.	7,367	Sept.	$38^3/4 – 39$	29	$37^5/8$
American Standard	2,500	Oct.	51	$30^1/2$	$73^1/4$
HRE Properties	117,500	Sept.	21	$17^1/4$	$23^5/8$
Rohm and Haas	25,000	Oct.	42	24	$33^3/8$
Schering Plough	2,000	Sept.	52	$31^1/4$	$53^1/2$
Smithkline Beckman	5,000	Sept.	$58^5/8$	$39^3/4$	58
U.S. Trust	5,000	Sept.	$43 – 44^3/4$	26	$45^1/2$

vested in their treasury stock are being put to better use than dollars invested in other instruments. Also, such purchases reduce the number of shares outstanding, thereby automatically increasing the profit per share of the reduced number of outstanding shares. The treasury stock can also be used to effect stock dividends or for acquisitions.

Before an investor decides whether to buy the stock, he should become aware of the price per share paid for the stock by the company. This can often be determined by reading the footnotes to the financial statements, which often provide details concerning the number of shares purchased and price per share. Another way to determine how much the company paid, but not always as accurate, is to deduct the number of shares of treasury stock of the prior year from the number shown for the current year (on the balance sheet) to determine the shares acquired in the current year. The same is done for the dollar cost, respectively. The number of shares acquired in the current year is then divided into their cost to determine the cost per share. This result is not always accurate; some of the shares purchased by the company in either year may have been used for corporate purposes, such as exercise of options by employees.

Two other matters concerning a company's purchase of treasury stock should be considered: If the stock was purchased at a price higher than the book value per share, it would often have a dilutive effect on equity (see ''Dilution—A Negative Fundamental Factor'' on p. 64.) A question might be asked: Why would a company do this? Such purchase might be made by a corporation because of assets (such as large acreages of land) that are still carried on its books at their original cost and that have substantially increased in value. The present book value per share of the company is, therefore, significantly undervalued.

RECORD OF DIVIDENDS—A Fundamental Factor

Fundamental analysts give weight to the record of earnings and dividend payouts of a company. A long history of increasing earnings per share and commensurate increases in dividends is considered a favorable factor in the selection of a stock for long-term investment.

A study of this kind produces widely varying philosophies by the management of companies regarding the payment of dividends. Many years ago, the then chairman of Crown Cork & Seal Company was known to have said: ''As long as I am head of this company we will never pay a dividend.'' To this day, that statement has been proven true.

In 1965 Crown Cork & Seal sold as low as 6^{7/8}$ per share. As this is written, its market price per share is $112. That stock has increased 1628% in value in 24 years.

Now let's refer to the stock dividend and stock splits as published in Core Industrials, Inc. report of Dividend Growth Record, as shown in Table 2-2.

Table 2-2 Core Industries Dividends

Record Date	Distribution
9/13/61	5%
9/12/62	5%
11/27/64	100%
3/07/67	10%
9/05/67	33$^{1/3}$%
3/05/68	10%
10/15/68	33$^{1/3}$%
2/26/73	100%
2/26/79	50%
2/26/80	50%
3/02/81	50%

Assume an investor bought 100 shares of stock of Core Industries Inc. on September 1, 1967 for a long-term investment. A cash dividend was paid on those shares in the amount of $54.50 during the year ended August 31, 1968. In each of the next 21 years, the cash dividends increased. During the year ended August 31, 1988, the cash dividends, resulting from stock dividends and splits, amounted to $863.54.

Core Industries Inc. dividends increased by about 1585% over a period of 21 years, as compared with an increase of 1628% in the market value of Crown Cork and Seal stock over 24 years.

Both companies are at opposite extremes with regard to the cash payment of dividends. One believes in rewarding investors with a cash return on a pay-as-you-go basis. The other believes that by withholding cash dividends and reinvesting earned profits in productive plant and equipment is the better policy in the longer term.

Regardless of the divergent dividend policies of Crown Cork and Seal and Core Industries, Inc., both companies illustrate how a long-term investment in the stock of a sound company can produce a cash return or an increase in the value of the stock—both of which exceed, by far, the rate of inflation, barring a major stock market crash and prolonged depression.

DILUTION—A Negative Fundamental Factor

Dilution means "reduction in strength." In the parlance of Wall Street, it represents a reduction in the value of the equity of a company.

In a business, there can be many causes of dilution. Some of these are listed below:

- When a company sustains a casualty not fully covered by insurance.

- When write-off of losses occur because of discontinued operations (plant shutdowns, obsolete product lines, and so on).

- When a large customer goes into bankruptcy and the company sustains a substantial bad debt.

- When stock options are exercised by directors, officers, or employees, which enables them to purchase common stock of the company at less cost than the book value per share.

- When goodwill is amortized.

- When the company loses an important lawsuit.

- When a company purchases its own stock at a market price higher than its book value.

- When, in this era or merger-mania, huge payouts are made to retiring or separated directors and/or officers of the bought-out company.

- When, again as a result of merger-mania, the company takes on huge junk bond indebtedness with virtually the same underlying assets. With these funds, the raiders are able to pay stockholders who accept the buy-out a substantially higher price for their stock than the previous prevailing market price per share.

Some of the above causes of dilution in a company's equity take effect immediately, while others require longer periods of time. Each of them have the effect of reducing the equity of a company and its book value per share of common stock outstanding. (*Note:* Book value per share is derived by dividing the net assets of a company—after deducting the stated or par or liquidation value of preferred stock, if any—by the number of shares of common stock outstanding.)

Many of the foregoing reasons for dilution in the net worth of a company are covered in current financial publications, the TV media, and in quarterly and/or annual reports of companies.

Whenever an investor notices potential dilution in a company's value, he should consider it a strong negative factor.

USING FUNDAMENTAL ANALYSIS

In chapter 1, technical analysis signals were given a purely subjective "value rating" on a scale of 1 to 10 (see p. 34). Here, we will attempt to do the same with several fundamental factors.

Please note from Table 2-3 that most fundamental factors can prove to be either positive or negative, while only a few can be strictly positive or negative ones.

None of the above fundamental analysis factors are considered to have a value rating of less than 8.

Generally, when a company is found to have either of the two "only negative" factors of dilution or excess of cost over value of net assets acquired, it is advisable to discard it from purchase consideration. This will eliminate a considerable number of companies, including those resulting from "merger mania," that make use of "junk bond" financing. At some future time, some of these companies will have to "pay the piper" and will wind up in financial trouble.

Inasmuch as there are a large number of factors and influences that may possibly affect the operations of a company, the larger the number of positive fundamental factors, the more qualified its stock becomes for potential purchase. (See also the worksheets at the end of the chapter.) However, we should then also consider technical signals. If they are flashing "red," the stock should only be placed on a potential buy list. When the technical signals flash "green," then reentering the market could prove beneficial.

PERCENTAGE OF NET PROFIT
TO SALES BY INDUSTRY GROUPS

The relative performance by industry in percentage of profits to sales could be a lead to a review of some companies in those industries. For example, refer to Table 4-2 on p. 103. You'll note that the paper and allied products industry was the only one showing increases in percent of profits to sales for four consecutive quarters ending September 30, 1977.

_____Table 2-3 Fundamental Factors_____

	Possible Factor		Value Rating	Page in Text
	Positive	Negative		
Working Capital Ratio	X	X	10	40
Excess of Cost over Value of Net Assets Acquired.........................		X	10	44
Cost of Goods Sold	X	X	10	47
Understanding Net Profits.............	X	X	10	48
Net Profit per Share Based Upon the Average Number of Shares Outstanding .	X	X	10	49
Sales Decrease vs. Cost of Goods Sold Decrease	X	X	10	50
Comparison of Profits to Sales with Prior Year or Quarter to Quarter	X	X	10	53
Decrease in Sales—Increase in Profits...........................	X		10	57
Insider Activity	X		10	59
Dilution		X	10	64
Merchandise Turnover	X	X	9	52
Stock Prices React to Earnings	X	X	9	53
Introduction of New Products..........	X		9	80
Debt to Equity Ratio	X	X	9	45
Company's Purchase of Treasury Stock	X	X	8	60
Record of Dividends	X		8	62
Ageing of Accounts Receivable.........	X	X	8	42
Percent of Net Profit to Sales by Industry Groups.....................	X	X	8	65

A comparison of the percent of net profits to sales of industries of 20 years ago, which had the same identifiable groupings as today, is shown in Table 2-4.

_____Table 2-4 Net Profit by Industry_____

	——Percent of Net Profit to Sales[1]——			
	1967		1987	
	2nd Qr.	3rd Qr.	2nd Qr.	3rd Qr.
Motor Vehicles & Equipment	6.3	1.9	6.2	4.7
Aircraft and Parts[2]	2.5	2.6	4.0	4.4
Nonferrous Metals	7.7	5.3	0.6	4.7
Rubber & Misc. Plastics Products	3.4	3.6	5.7	5.0
Instruments & Related Products	7.9	8.8	6.4	7.3
Textile Mill Products	2.7	2.9	3.2	4.5
Paper and Allied Products	4.9	4.5	5.6	6.4
Printing and Publishing	4.6	4.9	6.0	7.2
Drugs	2.3	2.4	12.7	12.8
Stone, Clay, and Glass Products	5.4	5.7	6.0	6.7
Iron and Steel	4.8	3.9	3.2	2.9

[1]Data extracted from 1967 and 1987 QFRs.
[2]1987 figures include guided missiles.

The Drug Industry shows the greatest percentage increase in Net Profits to Sales over a twenty year period.

FUNDAMENTAL ANALYSIS WORKSHEETS—
For Determining Positive or Negative
Fundamental Factors for any Company

Data gleaned from a balance sheet and a profit and loss statement can be used to determine fundamental factors, both positive and negative, of a company. Some of these factors can be ascertained by employing the following analyses:

Ageing of Accounts Receivable	Remarks
(1) $_____ amount of Sales divided by 12 equals average monthly sales of $_____.	If the amount of Accounts Receivable exceeds three times the average monthly Sales it could be a
(2) $_____ amount of Accounts Receivable divided by the average monthly sales of $_____ equals #_____.	negative factor.

Evaluation of the Collection Process:
To determine whether the collection of Accounts Receivable is improving or deteriorating, make a comparison of (1) and (2) above for two successive years and compare the average number of months of the age of the Accounts Receivable by years. An increase in months means deterioration; a decrease means improvement.

Working Capital Ratio	Remarks
$_____ amount of Current Assets divided by $_____ amount of Current Liabilities equals a ratio of _ to _.	A ratio of 2 to 1 or better is considered as positive.

Debt to Equity Ratio	Remarks
$_____ amount of Equity divided by $_____ amount of Debt equals a ratio of _ to _.	Generally, a ratio of 1 to 1 is fair; 3 to 2 is better; 3 to 1 is positive.

	Merchandise Turnover	**Remarks**

$\$$_____ amount of Sales of prior year added to

$\$$_____ amount of sales of current year equals $\$$_____ (A)

$\$$_____ amount of Merchandise Inventory of prior year added to

$\$$_____ amount of Merchandise Inventory of current year equals $\$$_____ (B)

$\$$_____ amount of (A) divided by

$\$$_____ amount of (B) equals average turnover rate of _____.

Remarks

Merchandise turnover rates should be compared with other companies in the same industry. Generally, the higher rate is considered as positive.

Sales Decrease vs. Cost of Goods Sold Decrease

(1) $\$$_____ amount of Sales of prior year

(2) $\$$_____ amount of Sales in current year deducted from prior year equals

(3) $\$$_____ amount of decrease in Sales

(3) divided by (1) equals the percentage decrease in Sales (%)

(4) $\$$_____ amount of Cost of Goods Sold in prior year

(5) $\$$_____ amount of Cost of Goods Sold in current year deducted from prior year equals

(6) $\$$_____ amount of decrease in Cost of Goods Sold

(6) divided by (4) equals the percentage decrease in Cost of Goods Sold

Remarks

A percentage decrease in Cost of Goods Sold which is greater than the percentage decrease in Sales is considered positive.

Return on Assets	Remarks
$_____ amount of Net Profits divided by	The percent of profits on Assets varies widely amongst industries. Banks strive to earn 2% on Total Assets. Industrial companies should earn a much higher return on Assets. In 1988 General Motor's return on Assets was approximately 4.8%.
$_____ amount of Total Assets equals the percentage return on Assets invested.	

Turnover Rate of Total Assets to Sales	Remarks
$_____ amount of Sales divided by	If this ratio is less than 1 to 1 much further analysis should be made before considering the stock for potential purchase.
$_____ amount of Total Assets equals the dollar amount of sales that each $1 invested in Assets can produce.	The higher the rate of dollars of Sales is to each $1 of Assets, the higher is the positive rating.

3

Other Investing Considerations

IN ADDITION TO TECHNICAL AND FUNDAMENTAL ANALYSES THERE ARE a number of investment considerations that may benefit investors in reaching investment decisions.

CORRELATION BETWEEN PRICE MOVEMENTS OF FIXED INTEREST INVESTMENTS AND CHANGES IN INTEREST RATES

It is a truism that fixed interest rate instruments such as bonds rise in price when interest rates fall, and drop when interest rates rise, and that, to a lesser degree, such changes affect interest-sensitive stocks, such as utilities and preferred stocks, as well as the general market. A rationale of why this relationship occurs again and again is offered here.

Numerous financial instruments are the means by which capital formation exists, such as common and preferred stocks and debenture and convertible bonds. The different kinds of financial instruments compete and vie for available investment dollars—always on a current interest-related basis. Let us explain by referring to a specific case.

On June 7, 1930 General Motors Corporation issued a 5% cumulative preferred stock with an "involuntary liquidation value of $100" per share, which provided a then-prevailing rate yield of 5%. A quarterly dividend rate of $1.25 has been paid on that preferred stock for over 59 years. The market price of the stock, however, fluctuates considerably. For example, during the period from 1971 to 1987, the price of the stock ranged between a high of $84 and a low of 36³/₄. Why?

If, at a given moment in time, vying instruments offer a $5 return for each $100 invested, the prevailing interest rate would be 5%. Now assume interest rates soared to 10%. All that would be required to earn the same $5 return would be to invest $50 in a vying instrument. All existing fixed-rate securities likewise react to such changes in interest rates by rising or falling in market prices.

A relationship of the market price of General Motors $5 preferred stock with the Federal Discount Rate is shown in Table 3-1.

Table 3-1 Discount Rate and G.M.'s $5 Pfd. Stock

Year	Discount Rate Range		Percent Range	Market Price General Motors $5 Pfd.		Dollar Range
	High	Low		High	Low	
1971	5¹/₄	4¹/₂	³/₄	84	73⁷/₈	10¹/₈
1972	5¹/₄	5¹/₄	-0-	82¹/₂	74¹/₂	8
1973	7¹/₂	5	2¹/₂	78¹/₂	68	10¹/₂
1974	8	7³/₄	¹/₄	71	55¹/₂	15¹/₂
1975	7¹/₄	6	1¹/₄	68³/₄	59	9³/₄
1976	5¹/₂	5¹/₄	¹/₄	74¹/₄	65	9¹/₄
1977	6	5³/₄	¹/₄	72³/₄	69¹/₈	3⁵/₈
1978	9¹/₂	6¹/₂	3	69	59¹/₄	9³/₄
1979	12	10	2	62³/₄	48³/₄	14
1980	13¹	10	3	54⁷/₈	41¹/₄	13⁵/₈
1981	14²	12	2	45³/₈	37	8³/₈
1982	11¹/₂	8¹/₂	3	49³/₄	36³/₄	13
1983	8¹/₂	8¹/₂	-0-	52¹/₈	43¹/₈	9
1984	9	8	1	52¹/₄	44¹/₄	8
1985	8	7¹/₂	¹/₂	58¹/₄	49	9¹/₄
1986	7¹/₂	5¹/₂	2	71³/₄	54³/₈	17³/₈
1987	6	5¹/₂	¹/₂	73¹/₄	49¹/₂	23³/₄

[1] Plus 3% Surcharge established for banks with total deposits of 500 million or more.

[2] Plus 4% Surcharge for frequent use by large borrowers.

The following shows the correlation between the major moves in the discount rate and the market prices of G.M. $5 preferred (pfd.) stock:

Years	Discount Rate	G.M. $5 Pfd.
1971 – 1974	Low 4^1/$_2$ to High 8	High 84 to Low 55^1/$_2$
1974 – 1976	High 8 to Low 3^3/$_4$	Low 59 to High 74^1/$_4$
1976 – 1981	Low 5^1/$_4$ to High 14	High 74^1/$_4$ to Low 37
1981 – 1987	High 14 to Low 5^1/$_2$	Low 36^3/$_4$ to High 73^1/$_4$

Other items of interest may be gleaned from Table 3-1.

The average annual price spread of the $5 pfd. stock of G.M. was 11 points. Only once in 17 years has the spread been lower than 5 and that was in year 1977 when it was 3^5/$_8$ points.

The next lowest spread of 8 points occurred in 1972 and 1984. Five times the spread was 9 or 9 and a fraction. Twice it was 10 and a fraction. It was 13 and a fraction twice and 14 twice. It was 15^1/$_2$, 17^3/$_8$, and 23^3/$_4$ once. In 1987, the year of the stock market crash, the spread was 23^3/$_4$.

The above may offer conservative investors a guide as to when to purchase or sell General Motor's $5 pfd. stock.

HIGH AND LOW PRICE SPANS OF STOCKS

Many newspapers and investment services publish the high and low range of market prices of stocks by calendar years or for 12 trailing months. If an investor can spare the time, he or she might make use of that published information. The stocks listed in Table 3-2 on p. 74 are intended for illustrative purposes only.

Correlating the current market price with the intrayear and inter-year highs and lows might suggest a stock purchase. If it appears the stock has a potential of a significant up-move, examining several other factors concerning that specific company would be prudent. For example, a further analysis of price changes, both down and up, and intrayear vs. interyear price relationships may prove beneficial:

		Loss		Loss		Loss
Present Value of Stock	100		100		100	
Drop in Price	25	25%	50	50%	75	75%
Price after drop	75		50		25	
		Gain		Gain		Gain
Present Value of Stock	75		50		25	
Gain in Price	25	33^1/$_3$%	50	100%	75	300%
Price after gain	100		100		100	

Table 3-2 High and Low Prices of Stocks

	1982	1983	1984	1985	1986	1987	Average all Years	Two Year Average
NCR Corp.								
H.	24	34	33	43	57	87	46	72
L.	10	21	21	25	39	49	27	44
Intrayear span	14	13	12	18	18	38	19	28
Interyear H. – L.	–	3	13	8	4	8	7	6
Interyear L. – H.	–	24	12	22	32	48	28	40
Motorola, Inc.								
H.	31	50	47	41	50	74	49	62
L.	16	27	29	29	34	35	28	34
Intrayear span	15	23	18	12	16	39	21	28
Interyear H. – L.	–	4	21	18	7	15	15	11
Interyear L. – H.	–	34	20	12	21	40	25	30
Westinghouse Electric								
H.	20	28	28	47	63	75	43	69
L.	11	19	20	25	42	40	26	49
Intrayear span	9	9	8	22	21	35	17	28
Interyear H. – L.	–	1	8	3	5	23	8	14
Interyear L. – H.	–	17	9	27	38	33	25	36

It is apparent from the above that the dollar drop in a stock represents a lower percentage loss than the percentage gain represented by the same amount of a dollar rise. Coupling this with the fact that the stock market trend over the years has been upward, the overall advantage lies with the buyer of stocks rather than with the seller.

Let's consider the stock of NCR. During the six years ending 1987 the stock rose from a low of 9$^7/_8$ to a high of 87. Remember that this period, before the crash in 1987, consisted of a great bull market.

A record of NCR's intra- and interyear percentage spans in price is furnished in the tabulation that follows. The stock prices have been rounded out to the nearest dollar.

	1982	1983	1984	1985	1986	1987	1988 to Nov. 4
Intrayear High	24	34	33	43	57	87	70
Intrayear Low	10	21	21	25	39	44	42
Intrayear downspan	14	13	12	18	18	43	28
% Down span	58%	38%	36%	42%	32%	49%	40%
Interyear High		34	33	43	57	87	70
Interyear Low	10	21	21	25	39	44	42
Interyear up span		24	12	22	32	48	26
% Up span		240%	57%	105%	128%	123%	59%

Doesn't the foregoing, with respect to NCR, point up that when its stock price is from 32% to 58% lower than its high of the year, it reflects a plus signal for possible acquisition, with the intention of holding the stock for a potential significant advance the following year?

Now let's analyze another stock, General Instrument:

	1982	1983	1984	1985	1986	1987	1988 to Nov. 4
Intrayear High	62	67	35	23	25	48	40
Intrayear Low	27	29	16	13	16	19	22
Intrayear downspan	35	38	19	10	9	29	18
% Down span	57%	57%	54%	44%	36%	60%	55%
Interyear High		67	35	23	25	48	40
Interyear Low	27	29	16	13	16	19	22
Interyear up span		40	6	7	12	32	21
% Up span		148%	17%	44%	92%	200%	111%

With respect to General Instrument, while the stock did very poorly in 1984, 1985, and 1986, of the five full years, only one inter-year low-to-high span was less than the intrayear span and one was even. The remaining three years showed substantial percentage inter-year span increases compared with intrayear percentage spans.

Another point to note is that for both NCR and General Instru-ment, the interyear high in the periods shown was never lower than the related intrayear low. In other words, if in a downtrend year in either stock, an investor could have spotted the near lows of the intrayears and held positions until the near highs of the following year, substantial gains could have been achieved.

Over a period of years, the price movements in a stock establish certain high and low spans. The investor might consider a stock for potential purchase when it falls near its average percentage declines and when a drop is coincident with a general market drop and not because of a negative factor unique to the company.

A word of caution here: In a recession or depression or decession (coined here: a *decession* is halfway between a recession and depres-sion), the above seemingly advantageous data can be diminished or eliminated.

MAJOR EVENTS AND THEIR IMPACT

It is universally recognized that the stock market generally reacts to unexpected events with volatile movement. A study of the impact on the stock market of a few such occurrences was made a number of years ago by Mr. Ralph A. Rotnem of Harris Upham & Co. (Table 3-3).[1]

The above study shows that when an unpredictable crisis occurs, the public realizes the situation may represent a serious problem, yet they find themselves unable to visualize possible consequences. As a result, they respond with a defensive posture. Often this mass psy-chology results in stampede selling of securities. This knee-jerk reac-tion then sets the stage for subsequent market recovery. As an example, follow the events shown in Table 3-3. No longer than $4^{1}/_{2}$ months were required to recover from 72% to 100% of the stock mar-ket losses. Does this not suggest that prudent investors should take advantage of lower prices generated by the above type of indiscrimi-nate selling and be in a position to benefit from the recovery?

---

[1]Table Courtesy of Harris Upham & Co.

_____Table 3-3 Unpredictable News and Stock Market Behavior_____

	DJI % loss	Days of Decline	Losses Recovered
Battleship Maine Sunk (1898)...........	$16^1/2$	32	100% in 36 days
San Francisco Earthquake (1906)........	11	14	82% in 26 days
Lusitania Sunk (1915)	11	32	100% in 16 days
Austrian Crisis (1938)	25	31	100% in 75 days
Munich Crisis (1938)..................	14	53	100% in 11 days
Czechoslovakian Crisis (1939)..........	22	24	100% in 130 days
Poland Invaded (1939)	7	17	100% in 9 days
Fall of France (1940)	25	26	72% in 127 days
Pearl Harbor (1941)...................	9	14	77% in 9 days
Berlin Crisis (1948)	9	72	82% in 18 days
Korean Crisis (1950)	$12^1/2$	13	100% in 43 days
President Eisenhower's Illness (1955)....	10	12	100% in 25 days
Cuban Crisis (1962)..................	$5^1/2$	6	100% in 6 days

EDSON GOULD'S THREE STEP AND STUMBLE RULE—A Warning of Impending Market Drop

The late Mr. Edson Gould, former editor of *Findings and Forecasts*, is credited for his "three step and stumble rule." He maintained that whenever the rates of one of three financial controls (discount rate, reserve requirement, or margin requirement) was increased three times consecutively, the stock market would fall badly after a three-month lag.

Fig. 3-1. Three Step and Stumble Rule: A Warning of Impending Market Drop
(Sketch by Holly Wilson-Perrotto)

The table below reflects the record after the three step and stumble rule was triggered by increases in the discount rate by the Federal Reserve.

Date	Previous Day Dow	Subsequent Drop in Dow Points
10/3/1919	118	44
7/13/1928	206	155
8/13/1948	179	17
9/9/1955	475	55
3/31/1959	602	65
12/6/1965	946	191
6/10/1968	909	278
5/4/1973	930	+80 then −430*

*Soon thereafter a long-term bull market commenced.

ONE WAY BIG MONEY IS MADE

To some, much of what appears in the foregoing pages may be old hat. They already possess extensive knowledge of Wall Street and deserve kudos. Others who may have found some of the material new and who understand the principles of fundamental and technical analyses and recognize their factors, signals, and indicators are probably equipped with more knowledge than a majority of the people who invest in the stock market.

If the reader makes use of the stock market principles discussed, he or she should, over the long haul, be successful. Of course, along the way, the investor will sustain losses. When that occurs, *the surest way to lose less* is to *cut and run*. Also, an investor should not fall in love with a stock as, unfortunately, so many people do.

The most difficult task an investment adviser has (aside from the inordinate amount of effort required in preparing a highly ethical and top-drawer investment letter) is to try to convince investors to sell stocks!

When using hard-earned money in investments, the tendency is toward conservatism. That makes it difficult to hit the jackpot. The really big money is made, however, by a relatively few number of investors and in a simple way. How is this done? First, by several individuals investing risk capital (for example $43,000) and receiving in return perhaps many thousands of shares of a company formed by them. The next step is to start a business operation and begin to show some profits and then sell themselves and their plans to an investment banker. Then go public.

One of the requirements of "going public" is to furnish a prospectus to interested investors, along with an admonition that it must be read before committing investment funds.

As a matter of self-protection a prospectus covering an impending new issue is generally couched in terms of warning: "This issue is speculative, the company has no product at this time" . . . "there is no assurance the company will be able to operate in the future" . . . "the company has not as yet operated at a profit" . . . "the company is engaging in a field replete with competition" . . . "there is no guarantee the company will be able to sell its services as planned," and so forth. In the past, such warnings have fallen on deaf ears and have had no effect on the public's rush for new securities.

Remember the data that was previously presented concerning the XYZ Company? Much of that information was patterned after an actual company. While some of the background information has not been made public, much can be deduced by piecing together some factors.

The company was formed in 1984 by a group of six or seven individuals who established a manufacturing facility to produce a number of products.

The Articles of Incorporation of the company, among other things, provided for the authorization of 10 million shares of common stock. The founders or insiders made purchases of 1,400,000 shares of common stock of 1 cent par value for $14,000, plus an additional amount of paid-in capital of about $287,000, for an average cost (if seven was the correct number of the company's founders) to each of approximately $43,000, resulting in a per share cost of 21.5 cents for 200,000 shares each.

Fortunately the products of the company were well received, and it earned profits much sooner than most newly formed organizations.

Now comes the big money! In 1985 the company made an initial public offering of about 932,000 shares of its authorized but unissued stock, resulting in an increase in outstanding stock valued at $9,320 and additional paid-in capital of $9,540,000.

In addition to the public offering, by exercising options, etc., the common stock outstanding increased to approximately 2,300,000 shares with 1 cent par value of $23,300, plus paid-in capital of approximately $9,820,000. These transactions, together with interim earnings and other relatively minor benefits, resulted in a substantial increase in book value to approximately $13,000,000.

The market price of the company's stock subsequently reached a high of $14. As this is written the current market price is $11 3/4. The 200,000 shares originally held by the founders at a cost of 21.5 cents per share currently have a market value of $2,350,000 for each investment of about $43,000.

Whenever potential investors are bombarded by peddlers of stock via the financial media, the number of shares owned by insiders and the price they paid for the stock is never mentioned. Often the number of shares in "float" is only a small portion of the outstanding shares; if the par value is 1 cent or 10 cents per share, it is an indication the insiders own a large chunk of the original issue and benefit from secondary issuances of the stock at much higher prices. Yet that does not mean the investor cannot still make a successful investment, even though it will come nowhere close to the benefits derived by the insiders.

INTRODUCTION OF NEW PRODUCTS

Being on the alert to an introduction of a new product, especially if it represents a "breakthrough-in-the-art," can prove of benefit to an investor. History has proven time and again that a new discovery, for instance, a new product or invention, often carries with it opportunity for substantial profit. Investors who recognize such potentials and have some risk capital to invest in them have often been financially rewarded. Here's one example:

In June 1965 an investor learned about Mohawk Data Sciences Corporation's new machine, the Data Recorder, by reading about it in a trade journal, *Electronic News*. He then thought about buying some of Mohawk's stock, which was selling at about $5 per share.

In those days, individuals familiar with computers and electronic data processing knew that for many years the highest cost of the then "advanced" systems was in having to keypunch and key-verify source data into tabulating cards and then having to feed the cards into a card-read machine to produce a magnetic tape for input to a computer system. Mohawk's data recorder was able to produce a magnetic tape right at its key console, thus bypassing the card preparation and card-read process. It was a breakthrough-in-the-art in data processing!

In early 1967 the investor actually saw some of Mohawk's installations in some of its customer's premises and he again thought about the possible purchase of its stock. At that time a secondary issue of Mohawk's stock was being offered at $20 per share. Mohawk's balance sheet, however, was not one to generate enthusiasm. Mohawk had more current liabilities than current assets. The company nonetheless had an excellent product with what seemed to be an almost unlimited potential. Still the investor made no purchase. Soon thereafter, while exiting an elevator in New York City, the investor noticed two large crates sitting in the hallway with the letters "MDS" stamped on them. The Mohawk Data Recorders had apparently been purchased by the company the investor was about to visit. That did it. As soon as the investor returned home he bought shares in MDS at $32 per share. From that day forward the stock advanced in price almost daily for some months. On some days the stock rose in price as much as $3 or $4 per share, and it continued to rise. When it reached $118, the investor sold his shares. His gain was 268% in 9 months!

The stock continued on its upward path, finally reaching $222 per share. In 1968 the stock was split 2 for 1. Following the split, when the stock sold about $100 per share, the demand for the company's data recorder was so intense, the company stubbed its toe and lost control of its operations. Allegedly, among other problems, the company could not adequately service all the machines in the hands of its customers. As a consequence the market price of the stock started a precipitous drop from around 100 and did not stop until it fell to under $2 a share in 1974.

The above was an outstanding example of a roller coaster ride of a stock. It spotlights the fact that no investor has ever made a profit without executing the "sell" side of a two-sided transaction.

THE M1 MONEY SUPPLY

For a considerable length of time, numerous stock market watchers eagerly waited each week for release of the M1 figures (cash in banks and checking account balances).

While the impact of the rise and fall in M1 on inflation, deflation, the economy, and the stock market has not always been consistent, from 1982 to 1987 the money supply growth was associated with a huge rise in the stock market (see Fig. 3-2). Then, after the growth rate was tightened with a rise in the discount rate on September 14, 1987, the second biggest crash in the stock market soon followed.

Figure 3-3 shows the correlation between the real M1 money supply and the real S&P 400 Industrial Index from 1960 through the crash in October 1987.

(NOTE: In essence, "real rates" are considered equal to "Nominal Rates" minus the "Inflation Rate.")

CALLABLE PROVISIONS OF PREFERRED STOCK AND BONDS

Some investors, unaware of the callable (redeemable) provisions of their income securities such as preferred stock or bonds, have been

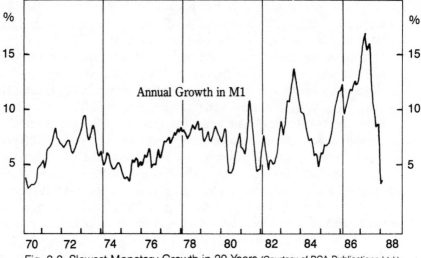

Fig. 3-2. Slowest Monetary Growth in 20 Years (Courtesy of BCA Publications Ltd.)

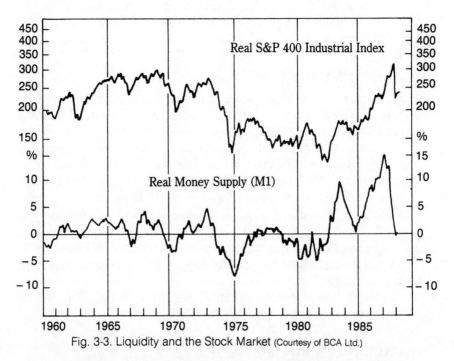

Fig. 3-3. Liquidity and the Stock Market (Courtesy of BCA Ltd.)

subject to sudden losses. If the market price of a security is higher than its redeemable value, the price will fall to that value if it is called-in by the company (Fig. 3-4).

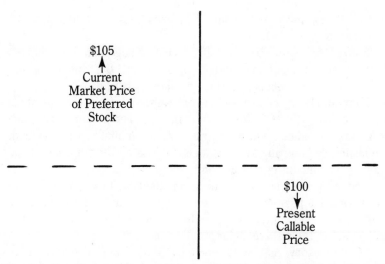

$105
↑
Current
Market Price
of Preferred
Stock

$100
↓
Present
Callable
Price

Fig. 3-4. Knowledge of Current Price vs. Callable Provisions can be Advantageous

A case in point is found in the $4.18 preferred stock of Central Louisiana Electric. The stock sold at $38 a share, while paying $4.18 in dividends for an annual "yield" of 11%—which seemed like an attractive investment. However, let's dig a little beneath the surface. At the time of purchase, the stock was callable at $30.29 per share until August 31, 1987. After August 31, 1987 the stock was callable at $28.89 per share.

To earn the 11% yield would require holding the stock for about a year to obtain the four quarterly dividends of $1.045 per quarter.

The last dividend payment of $1.045 was made on September 1, 1987. Anyone who bought the stock at or near the top of $38 was subject (at the option of the company) to an immediate redemption at $30.29 per share, and after August 31, 1987, at $28.89 per share. The buyer could have sustained a loss in capital invested of over 15%.

Any good broker has information regarding the callability of fixed-income securities. Investors should inquire whether their holdings are redeemable and, if so, the dates they are effective and their redemption price.

THE EFFECT OF DIVIDEND CAPTURE TRADES

A relatively new practice has been developed between some Japanese insurance companies and certain brokerage firms that allegedly violates certain rules of the stock exchange and its "public outcry auction system." The result has, intermittently, affected the validity of the

"Arms" index and other technical indexes that are relied upon by some investors.

A *dividend capture trade* is one in which a huge number of shares are purchased on a high-dividend paying stock, and the broker sells the stock "short" for delivery on the "dividend record date."

Moments later, the broker "covers his short" by buying the stock back for delivery the day after the record date. The broker's sale price of the stock is adjusted upward to cover the amount of the dividend. The insurance company sustains a capital loss on the transaction and receives the amount of the dividend.

Under Japanese law, companies can offset capital gains, which are not allowed for payment of dividends, by the capital loss sustained from the dividend capture trade. The dividend income they capture can be paid to their shareholders in dividends.

On Wednesday, August 4, 1988 a block of 50 million shares (more than 25% of the 193,535,000 shares outstanding) of American Electric Power Corp. was purchased to capture the dividend of record the following day. The dividend was 58 cents plus 5 cents extra per share, amounting to $31,500,000. Many other such trades have occurred including one for more than 20% of the outstanding stock of SCE Corp.

The rules covering short sales require the ability of the broker to borrow the stock from a third party, if the required amount is not otherwise available for sale, for delivery to the purchaser.

Huge trades like those mentioned have aroused the suspicion that they have been executed without the broker being able to borrow the stock. Thus, it is believed the transfer of stock certificates does not occur, and such trades represent a bookkeeping transaction only.

Now let's consider how dividend capture trades affect the Arms Index (see page 115). Assume the stock involved is trading at the same price as at the close of the previous day. The broker and the Japanese strike a deal for the stock to be purchased at the same price, and minutes later it is sold at the same price with the short seller and the subsequent buyer being the broker. At that moment the Arms Index would not be affected at all. Let's further assume a few minutes later there were several small trades of the public of a few hundred or so shares, and the price of the stock rose $1/4$ of a point. This would trigger a very dramatic move in the Arms Index from, say, 1.30 (bearish) to .20 (very bullish). The opposite would occur in the event the public's trades moved the price lower than the dividend capture trade. Worse, the Arms Index could then swing from bullish to bearish and back and forth several times a day.

The foregoing situation cries aloud for remedial action, which may have begun. The New York Stock Exchange now makes the dividend capture trades more difficult by requiring the insurance companies to put up front and overnight the cash required for the purchase. Also the Japanese government has "requested" the insurance companies to discontinue the practice. Reports hold that a handful of such companies have agreed to stop while others will continue with the trades.

The New York Stock Exchange or the SEC should require that such trades be considered private transactions separate from the Exchange and not be entered into the stock trading computer system.

THE DOW INDUSTRIALS-DIVIDEND RATIO
SIGNAL—An Important Consideration

On a number of occasions the Dow Industrials Ratio signal has demonstrated convincing evidence that when the dividends on the Dow Industrials reach a high level, the stock market as a whole is at or near a low point. Conversely, when the Dow Industrial dividend yield was at a low level, the market was near a peak.

The lowest price reached by the Dow Industrials since 1916 occurred in 1932 when it reached a bottom of 40.6. At that time the Dow Industrials-Dividend Ratio was 14 to 1 (reciprocal of $7^2/7\%$ yield). The highest ratio was 39.3 to 1 (reciprocal of 2.53% yield), which coincided with the top of the market when it reached 2742 in 1987 (Fig. 3-5).

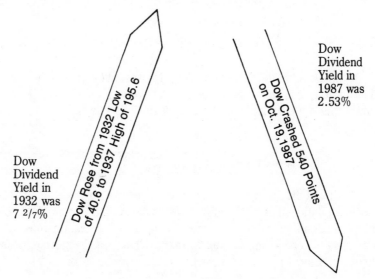

Fig. 3-5. Dividend Yield Signals are Important Considerations

This signal seems to tell us that even over a time span of 71 years, dividends paid are an important consideration of John Q. Public when investing funds in stocks. A number of times over the years, when the Dow Industrials yields produced a return of 6 to 7²/₇%, demand for stocks increased with a commensurate rise in stock prices. On the other hand, when, over a number of years and on a number of occasions, stock prices reached a point where the yield dropped to 4% or less, the demand lessened and the market subsequently dropped.

Since the year 1920 the lowest ratio of the Dow Industrials to its dividends was 12.2 to 1, which occurred in 1950 when the Dow sank to the area of 195 and its dividends were $16.16. This produced a record-high yield of 8.2%.

Also, since 1920 the highest ratio of the Dow to its dividends was 39.1 to 1, which occurred in 1987 when the Dow reached 2742 and its dividends were $69.50. This produced a record-low yield of $2.53%.

Hypothesis: The Dow reached its high to date of 2810.15 on January 3, 1990 and its dividends were $106.74. Assuming the record-low yield of 2.5% again comes into play, how high from 2810 could the Dow reach?

$$
\begin{array}{r}
2810 \\
\times\ 2.53 \\
\hline
71.093
\end{array}
$$
    Factor to determine how high the Dow
    may go based upon the 2.5% return
    of dividends of $106.74

$$2810.15 \times \frac{106.74}{71.093} \approx$$ Hypothetical high of
                               4219.19 for the Dow

If the Dow reaches a high of 4219.19, assuming dividends rise to $110 and the historical high percent return of dividends of 8.2% again occurs, the Dow could drop to a low as shown below:

$$110 \div 2810.15 \approx .039$$

$$2810.15 \times \frac{.039}{.082} \approx$$ Hypothetical low of 1336.52
                            for the Dow

It should be recognized the above correlations represent the extreme relationships of the high and low of the Dow to the high and low of dividend yields on the Dow. Such extreme relationships have occurred only once each in over 70 years. Therefore, something short of such relationships would most likely occur in the future.

PRICE TO EARNINGS RATIO

As described herein, there are many kinds of bookkeeping entries and other factors that can and do have a direct effect on the amount of "profits per share" as reported by companies.

Some investors, as well as technical and fundamental analysts are aware of numerous signals, factors, influences, and indicators that are used in stock market decision making. Yet the one that is undoubtedly known and used most by investors is the *PE* (price to earnings) *Ratio*.

With "profits per share" being one of the two components of this ratio, it should be recognized that if the company's accounting practices are consistent from year to year, more reliance can be placed on comparisons of year to year ratios of "price to earnings." The investor is advised of this by the wording contained in the Independent Accounting Firm's Certification found in the company's annual report which generally states: ". . . these financial statements present fairly the financial position of the company . . . in conformity with generally accepted accounting principles consistently applied . . . " If a change in accounting practice occurs, the accountants will add a comment such as ". . . except for the change in the pricing of inventories from first in/first out to last in/first out and in the changes in the rates of depreciation, with which we concur."

It has been said many times that human nature doesn't change; however, a significant change in the perspective of investors has occurred.

Some years back, a major consideration of investors was the percentage return on investment through the payment of dividends. For many years investors attempted to search out and invest in companies having a price to earnings ratio of 10 to 1 or less, and with a dividend payout rate of 50% of earnings. Today we find that the ratio may be 20 to 1 and even higher. With a 50% dividend payout policy, the contrast between today and yesteryear is shown below:

	P:E Ratio	*Percent of Earnings to Market Price*	*50% Dividend Representing Return on Market Price of Stock*
Yesteryear	10-1	10%	5%
Today	20-1	5%	2.5%

Because of the rate of growth of companies, there seems to be some partial justification for the above change that has taken place.

But when the pendulum swings too far in the deterioration of dividend return, the investor should be on guard. (Refer back to section entitled ''The Dow Industrials—Dividend Ratio Signal'' on p. 85).

60 YEARS OF DOW JONES INDUSTRIALS (1929 – 1988)

A wealth of data concerning the high and low points of the Dow Industrials covering a 60-year period can be gleaned from Table 3-4.

While studying the table, note the following:

1. The Dow hit more lows during the first six months of the years than in the last six months (38 to 22).

2. The Dow hit more highs in the last six months of the years than in the first six months (39 to 21).

3. In only one of 60 years, the Dow hit a high in August (year 1987).

4. In only one of 60 years, the Dow hit a low in August (year 1982).

5. More lows (19) were hit in the month of January than in any other month.

6. More highs (18) were attained in December than in any other month.

Now, using the historical record as a guide, how can some of the data on the chart be put to use based upon probabilities of chance? Let's assume:

If the Dow is at or near a new low (so far in the year) in the month of:

- *July*, the chances are 19 to 3 the Dow will hit a lower low in August, September, October, November, or December.

- *August*, the chances are 18 to 1 the Dow will hit a lower low in September, October, November, or December.

- *September*, the chances are 16 to 2 the Dow will hit a lower low in October, November, or December.

- *October*, the chances are 11 to 5 the Dow will hit a lower low in November or December.

- *November*, the chances are 6 to 5 the Dow will hit the yearly low in December.

Table 3-4 Sixty Years of Dow Jones Industrials (1929 – 1988)

	Dow High	Dow Low Months and Number of Times											
Months	Number of Times	Jan	Feb	Mar	Apr	May	Jun	Jul	Aug	Sep	Oct	Nov	Dec
January	8						2	1		1	1	1	2
February	3							1			1	1	1
March	3							1				1	1
April	4 (21)	1								1			1
May	2										1		1
June	1			1									
July	5	2	1			1					1		
August	1										1		
Sept.	6 (39)	3	1		1							1	
October	2	1										1	
November	7	4		2	1								
December	18	8	3	1	1	2	2		1				
	60	19	5	4	3	3	4	3	1	2	5	5	6

(38) (22)

Continued

Table 3-4 Continued

Dow Low		Dow High Months and Number of Times											
Months	Number of Times	Jan	Feb	Mar	Apr	May	Jun	Jul	Aug	Sep	Oct	Nov	Dec
January	19 ⎫				1			2		3	1	4	8
February	5 ⎪							1		1			3
March	4 ⎬ 38						1					2	1
April	3 ⎪									1		1	1
May	3 ⎪							1					2
June	4 ⎭	2											2
July	3 ⎫	1	1	1									
August	1 ⎪			1									
Sept.	2 ⎬ 22	1	1		1								
October	5 ⎪	1		1		1		1	1	1	1		
November	5 ⎪	1			1	1		1		1			
December	6 ⎭	2	1	1	1	1							1
	60	8	3	3	4	2	1	5	1	6	2	7	18
		⎩———— 21 ————⎭						⎩———— 39 ————⎭					

39

If the Dow is at or near a new high (so far in the year) in the month of:

- *July*, the chances are 34 to 5 the Dow will achieve a higher high in August, September, October, November, or December.

- *August*, the chances are 33 to 1 the Dow will achieve a higher high in September, October, November, or December.

- *September*, the chances are 27 to 6 the Dow will achieve a higher high in October, November, or December.

- *October*, the chances are 25 to 2 the Dow will achieve a higher high in November or December.

- *November*, the chances are 18 to 7 the Dow will achieve the yearly high in December.

STOCK MARKET CYCLES

Many investors believe the stock market repeats itself in time frames or patterns. One theory is based upon the "waves" principle. Another is predicated upon cycles that span decades.

To search out further proof of repetitive occurrences in the market, let's select for our time frame the 60-year period of 1930 through 1989.

First, a study was made to determine the up and down trends of the Dow Industrials in each 3rd, 4th, 5th, 6th, 7th, 8th, 9th, and 10th year cycle, starting with the year 1930, which consisted of a total of 480 different cycles. Next, the years were grouped into three-year cycles.

Note from Table 3-5 that nothing of particular importance can be reported with respect to the 60 three-year cycles since the year 1930. However, Table 3-5 is given as an example of the manner in which the uptrend and downtrend by years was recorded. Similar tables were prepared for each of the other cycle years, but only those containing significant data are provided herein.

(Little of importance was found with respect to the 60 four-year cycles.)

Refer to Table 3-6 for details of the 60 five-year cycles. Note that of the 12 five-year cycles started in 1933, the Dow trend was up in 10 years and down in two. The next such five-year cycle will come in 1993. However, a conclusion that 1993, or any other year, will be an up year should not be based upon any *one* cycle or any other single factor. A number of different cycles end in each year beginning in 1990. (A summary of all past cycles, covered in the study, which will next occur in the years 1990 through 1999 is provided in Table 3-9.)

_____Table 3-5 Dow Industrials Every 3rd Year_____

Downtrend	Uptrend	Down	Up
1930, 57, 60, 66, 69, 81, 84, 87	1933, 36, 39, 42, 45, 48, 51, 54, 63, 72, 75, 78	8	12
1931, 34, 37, 40, 46, 73, 79	1943, 49, 52, 55, 58, 61, 64, 67, 70, 76, 82, 85, 88	7	13
1932, 41, 53, 62 71, 74, 77	1935, 38, 44, 47, 50, 56, 59, 65, 68, 80, 83, 86, 89	7	13
		22	38

_____Table 3-6 Dow Industrials Every Fifth Year_____

Downtrend	Uptrend	Down	Up
1930, 40, 60	1935, 45, 50, 55, 65, 70, 75, 80, 85	3	9
1931, 41, 46, 66, 71, 81	1936, 51, 56, 61, 76, 86	6	6
1932, 37, 57, 62, 77, 87	1942, 47, 52, 67, 72, 82	6	6
1953, 73	1933, 38, 43, 48, 58, 63, 68, 78, 83, 88	2	10
1934, 69, 74, 79 84	1939, 44, 49, 54, 59, 64, 89	5	7
		22	38

(Nothing of significance can be reported concerning the 60 six-year cycles.)

As you can see in Table 3-7, the seven-year cycles that commenced in 1933 produced an uptrend in the Dow in eight years and a downtrend in only one. The next such cycle year is 1996. It should

_____Table 3-7 Dow Industrials Every 7th Year_____

Downtrend	Uptrend	Down	Up
1930, 37, 79	1944, 51, 58, 65, 72, 86	3	6
1931, 66, 73, 87	1938, 45, 52, 59 80	4	5
1932, 46, 53, 60, 74, 81	1939, 67, 88	6	3
1940	1933, 47, 54, 61, 68, 75, 82, 89	1	8
1934, 41, 62, 69	1948, 55, 76, 83	4	4
1977, 84	1935, 42, 49, 56 63, 70	2	6
1957, 71	1936, 43, 50, 64 78, 85	2	6
		22	38

also be noted, as shown in Table 3-9, that the total of the several cycle years, next occurring in 1996, produced the second-highest combined percentage (73.3%) of uptrend years.

(Nothing deserving special consideration could be gleaned from the eight- or nine-year cycles.)

Note in Table 3-8 that in all six of the 10-year cycles where the last digits of the years ended in "5" and also in "8," the Dow was in an uptrend. Also of interest is that in 11 of those 12 years, the lows in the Dow were reached in the first three months; in nine of the 12 years, the highs were reached in the last three months. Also, 11 highs occurred in the last six months of the years and all lows in the first six months.

Now refer ahead to Table 3-9, which shows the 10-year cycle ending in "8" was part of the several combined cycles, which will next occur in 1998, and which produced the highest percentage (76.9%) of uptrend years of all the combined groupings.

SUMMARY OF 480 DOW INDUSTRIAL CYCLES

A summary of the up and down trends of the 480 cycles included in the study is reflected in Table 3-9. Table 3-9 also shows when each cycle will next occur in the years 1990 through 1999.

Table 3-8 Dow Industrials Every Tenth Year

Downtrend	Uptrend	Down	Up
1930, 40, 60	1950, 70, 80	3	3
1931, 41, 71, 81	1951, 61	4	2
1932, 62	1942, 52, 72, 82	2	4
1953, 73	1933, 43, 63, 83	2	4
1934, 74, 84	1944, 54, 64	3	3
	1935, 45, 55, 65, 75, 85	0	6

Low		High		Upspan
3/14/35	96.11	11/19/35	148.44	51.73
1/24/45	151.35	12/11/45	195.82	44.47
1/17/55	388.20	12/30/55	488.40	100.20
6/28/65	840.59	12/31/65	969.24	128.65
1/ 2/75	632.04	7/15/75	881.81	249.77
1/ 4/85	1184.96	12/16/85	1553.10	368.14

1946, 66	1936, 56, 76 86	2	4			
1937, 57, 77 87	1947, 67,	4	2			
	1938, 48, 58, 68, 78, 88	0	6			
1969, 79	1939, 49, 59 89	2	4			

3/31/38	98.95	11/12/38	159.51	60.56
3/16/48	165.39	6/15/48	193.16	27.77
2/25/58	436.89	12/31/58	586.65	149.76
3/21/68	825.13	12/ 3/68	985.21	160.08
2/28/78	742.12	9/ 8/78	907.74	165.62
1/20/88	1879.14	10/21/88	2183.50	304.36

Table 3.9 Summary of Dow Cycles

Ending in Calendar Year	3rd		4th		5th		6th		7th		8th		9th		10th		Total		%	
	Down	Up	Down	Up	Down	Up	Down	Up	Down	Up	Down	Up	Down	Up	Down	Up	Down	Up	Down	Up
1990	8	12	6	9	3	9	4	6	4	4	3	4	1	5	3	3	32	52	38.1	61.9
1991	7	13	4	11	6	6	4	6	2	6	0	7	3	3	4	2	30	54	35.7	64.3
1992	7	13	4	11	6	6	3	7	2	6	2	5	1	5	2	4	27	57	32.1	67.9
1993			8	7	2	10	4	6	3	6	4	3	4	3	2	4	27	39	40.9	59.1
1994					5	7	3	7	4	5	3	5	2	5	3	3	20	32	38.5	61.5
1995							4	6	6	3	4	4	3	4	0	6	17	23	42.5	57.5
1996									1	8	2	6	3	4	2	4	8	22	26.7	73.3
1997											4	4	2	5	4	2	10	11	47.6	52.4
1998													3	4	0	6	3	10	23.1	76.9
1999															2	4	2	4	33.3	66.7
																	176	304		

Based upon historical cycle performance, the best chance of an uptrend year in the 1990s will be in 1998, which has the highest combined group percentage rating of 76.9%. The next-highest combined cycle percentage rating of 73.3% applies to the year 1996. The poorest chance of an uptrend year would occur in 1997, with a combined group percentage rating of only 52.4%.

"Percent Return on Equity"— A Misleading Phrase?

THOSE WHO ARE SAVVY IN THE JARGON OF WALL STREET ARE AWARE OF the limited valid usage of the phrase "percent return on equity." For a few the expression can be of use. If an entrepreneur wants to start a business, his or her knowledge of the "percent return on equity" by others in the same kind of business could be helpful. The same applies to the management of competitive companies. It could mean something to those who founded a company and were able to purchase or acquire shares of its stock at or less than its book value per share, and to those who, in rare cases, find companies whose per share book value is as high as the market price per share.

Because of its limited practical usage, shouldn't the general public be on guard with respect to any quoted "percent return on equity"? To an unwitting listener this expression might imply a high return for the investor on a suggested investment. After all, this term is used so often by those who suggest a stock for purchase in the financial press or via investment programs on TV, yet who are aware that such percentage is much higher than an investor would normally receive on an investment.

For John Q. Public the statement "percent return on equity" is a non sequitur and completely removed from being punctilious.

Table 4-1 Percent Return on Equity vs. Cost
May 6. 1988

Company	Book Value	Earnings Per Share	"Percent Return on Equity"	Cost at Market Price	Return on Market Price Cost	Cash Dividend	Dividend % Yield
Esselite Business Systems, Inc.	$21.35	$2.79	13.1%	37¹/₄	7.5%	$.88	2.4%
Martin Marietta Corp.	16.71	4.25	25.4%	43¹/₄	9.8%	1.05	2.5%
Fay's Drug Company, Inc.	3.90	.29	7.5%	8³/₄	3.3%	.20	2.3%
Liz Clairborne, Inc.	4.11	1.32	32.1%	15	8.8%	17	1.1%
Chemed Corp.	14.82	1.60	10.8%	34	4.7%	1.72	5.1%
House of Fabrics	14.12	1.58	11.2%	18¹/₈	8.7%	.48	2.6%
RTE Corp.	14.14	2.21	15.6%	41	5.4%	.68	1.8%

If a company earned, say, $6 per share and its book value per share is $40, it would have a 15 percent return on equity. Then, if it paid 50% of its earnings in dividends, or $3, the "return" would be 7.5%. Right? Sure, but only to those who had purchased the stock at its book value of $40. Moreover, let's assume that an investor purchases the company's stock at its current market price of $60 a share. The $3 dividend would then represent a 5% return on his investment while the 15% return on equity remains the same. (The market price per share can be double or triple the book value per share.) On January 12, 1990 when the Dow Industrials was 2,689.21, such market price of the 30 stocks was 250.4% higher than their book values, totalling $1075.49.

The following comments are offered to investors who are not familiar with the many factors that can affect the dollar amount reported as "return on equity." Although this term is used in condensed financial data regarding specific companies and published weekly, the investor should be aware of possible pitfalls if he or she gives more than a minor consideration to "return on equity" in making a stock selection. Table 4-1 shows the differences between the percent return on equity and the present return on the market price per share of several companies.

QFR BOOKLET

The *Quarterly Financial Report (QFR) for Manufacturing, Mining, and Trade Corporations* contains, among other quarterly financial statistics, income statements, and balance sheets covering 170 pages. Published by the U.S. Department of Commerce, Bureau of the Census, these statements consolidate the financial figures for 7,692 manufacturing corporations, 650 corporations in retail trade, 1,092 corporations in wholesale trade, and 302 corporations in mining, all of which represents QFR's universe sample.[1] In addition, income statements and balance sheets are consolidated by industry groups and size of corporations within the four major groups.

The purpose of the report is quoted from the QFR:

Purpose of Report: The main purpose of the QFR is to provide timely, accurate data on business financial conditions for use by Government and private sector organizations and individuals. Among its users, the Commerce Department regularly employs QFR data as an important component in determining corporate profits for GNP and National income estimates; the Federal Reserve Board uses the QFR to assess

---

[1]The QFR can be purchased for $20 per year, or $5 per single copy.

industrial debt structure, liquidity, and profitability; the Treasury Department estimates corporate tax liability through use of QFR data; the Council of Economic Advisors and Congressional Committees utilize key indicators derived from QFR data as they design economic policies and draft legislation; the Federal Trade Commission (FTC) utilizes the series as a basic reference point in analyzing the financial performance of American industries; and banking institutions *and financial analysts draw upon the series in making investment evaluations.* [Italics added.]

In the event an investor has tentatively selected a stock for purchase, he or she may wish to review the QFR to ascertain whether the company is faring better or worse than the sum total of all the companies in its applicable industry.

For Example:

Table 4-2, adapted from Table B in the QFR, reflects profits per dollar of sales by division and major group.

Hundreds of industry-wide balance sheets contain:

- Net working capital

- Selected balance sheet ratios:

Total cash, U.S.
Government, and other securities
Trade Accounts and trade notes receivable
Inventories
Total current assets
Net property, plant, and equipment
Short-term debt including
installments on long-term debt
Total current liabilities
Long-term debt
Total liabilities
Stockholders' equity

Ratios as
percent of
Total
Assets

Hundreds of Industry-wide Income Statements contain:

- Annual rate of profit on stockholders
  equity at end of period:

  Before income taxes
  After taxes

- Annual rate of profit on total assets:

  Before income taxes
  After taxes

See previous and later
comments regarding the
expression "Annual rate
of profit on stockholders'
equity."

Table 4-2 Profits per Dollar
of Sales by Division and Major Group
(Excerpt from Table B of QFR, used with permission)

Industry	Income before income taxes					Income after income taxes				
	3Q 1986	4Q 1986	1Q 1987	2Q 1987	3Q 1987	3Q 1986	4Q 1986	1Q 1987	2Q 1987	3Q 1987
All manufacturing corporations	5.6	5.1	6.8	8.0	8.2	3.4	3.3	4.3	5.3	5.6
Nondurable manufacturing corporations	7.0	6.8	7.6	8.4	9.4	4.3	4.5	5.1	5.6	6.2
Food and kindred products	6.2	8.1	5.9	7.1	6.7	3.9	5.2	3.7	4.4	4.4
Tobacco manufactures	NA	NA	NA	NA	NA	NA	NA	NA	NA	NA
Textile mill products	6.8	7.7	5.8	5.6	6.8	3.7	4.4	3.4	3.2	4.5
Paper and allied products	6.9	8.2	8.3	9.3	10.2	4.3	4.8	5.0	5.6	6.4
Printing and publishing	12.7	11.8	8.0	10.2	11.7	7.3	7.2	4.6	6.0	7.2
Chemicals and allied products	11.9	7.0	12.5	10.6	15.5	7.5	4.3	8.2	7.1	10.1
Industrial chemicals and synthetics	8.8	5.4	10.8	11.7	18.3	5.8	2.8	7.1	7.6	11.2
Drugs	25.0	22.3	20.9	18.0	18.4	15.8	16.7	14.6	12.7	12.8
Petroleum and coal products	1.1	2.5	6.2	9.0	8.2	0.7	2.9	5.2	7.1	7.1
Rubber and miscellaneous plastics products	8.7	3.9	7.8	8.0	7.3	5.5	1.9	5.6	5.7	5.0
Other nondurable manufacturing corporations	4.0	5.8	4.8	2.2	5.5	2.0	3.7	3.0	0.8	3.8
Durable manufacturing corporations	4.2	3.5	5.9	7.5	7.1	2.4	2.2	3.6	5.0	4.9
Stone, clay and glass products	7.4	7.9	8.2	9.3	9.7	4.6	4.4	5.4	6.0	6.7
Primary metal industries	-8.7	-0.6	4.2	4.0	5.6	-9.5	-1.4	2.9	2.0	3.7
Iron and steel	-17.9	-3.2	3.8	4.9	4.2	-18.8	-4.0	2.9	3.2	2.9
Nonferrous metals	2.4	2.7	4.8	4.9	7.1	1.7	2.9	2.9	0.6	4.7
Fabricated metal products	4.7	3.9	3.6	6.5	6.4	2.4	2.1	1.7	4.0	4.4
Machinery, except electrical	5.0	4.3	3.6	8.5	7.7	3.3	2.7	1.5	6.0	5.4
Electrical and electronic equipment	5.2	4.8	6.8	7.7	7.3	3.2	4.0	4.2	4.8	4.8
Transportation equipment	4.1	2.8	7.1	7.7	5.7	3.1	2.1	4.7	5.3	4.5
Motor vehicles and equipment	3.4	3.8	8.1	8.8	5.2	2.9	3.5	5.6	6.2	4.7
Aircraft, guided missiles and parts	5.4	1.1	6.0	6.1	6.6	3.6	-0.2	3.8	4.0	4.4
Instruments and related products	9.0	-1.7	9.6	9.8	10.6	6.1	-2.9	6.3	6.4	7.3
Other durable manufacturing corporations	6.0	6.0	5.3	7.8	7.4	3.6	3.5	2.9	4.8	4.8
All mining corporations	-13.6	-15.6	-3.1	-3.3	1.8	-12.9	-14.2	-4.3	-5.9	-0.2
All retail trade corporations	3.6	6.3	2.6	3.5	NA	2.0	3.6	1.5	2.1	NA
All wholesale trade corporations	1.8	2.4	1.9	1.8	2.2	0.9	1.3	1.2	1.0	1.4

If the investor has not yet made stock selections, he or she might seek out in the QFR those industries whose results are relatively better than others. Further analysis would then be required by referring to a financial service such as Value Line, which identifies and groups companies by industry and furnishes detailed financial data for each individual company.

In considering the widespread use made of QFR by many governmental agencies as well as industry and the public, a word of caution is advisable here. Unless all of the six-page Introduction of QFR has been carefully read and understood, the published figures of "Annual Rate of Profit on Stockholders' Equity, By Division and Major Group" could readily be misleading.

The following is quoted from page xii of QFR.

1. Annual Rate of Profit on Stockholders' Equity at End of Period. This ratio is obtained by multiplying income for the quarter before or after domestic taxes (including branch income (loss) and equity in the earnings of nonconsolidated subsidiaries net of foreign taxes) by four, to put it on an annual basis, and then dividing by stockholders' equity at the end of the quarter. *It measures the rate of return which accrues to stockholders on their investment.* [Italics supplied.]

2. Annual Rate of Profit on Total Assets. This ratio is obtained by multiplying income, as defined in deriving the rate of profit on stockholders' equity, both before and after taxes, by four, and then dividing by total assets at the end of the quarter. This ratio measures the productivity of assets in terms of producing income.

It gives me no pleasure to say what I'm about to say, but I feel it is imperative, especially in a book whose subject matter is how to invest successfully.

Refer to Tables 4-3, 4-4, and 4-5, adapted from QFR Tables 47.0, 47.1, and D, respectively. The line on Table 4-3 with the upper arrow (which has been added) shows the income after taxes by quarter for 650 corporations in the retail trade, and the line with the bottom (added) arrow shows the "annual rate of profit on stockholders' equity at end of period, after taxes." These figures are also shown on Table D covering all industries. In Table 4-4, the line with the added arrow shows the stockholders' equity for corporations in the retail trade.

The methodology used in the QFR to derive the annual rate of return on stockholders's equity is shown below. The figures used are those of the corporations in the retail trade.

	1986		1987	
	3rd Qr. Earnings	4th Qr. Earnings	1st Qr. Earnings	2nd Qr. Earnings
	Million Dollars			
Actual Earnings	$ 2,471	$ 5,064	$ 1,766	$ 2,663
Multiplied by	4	4	4	4
	$ 9,884	$20,256	$ 7,064	$10,652
Divided by actual equity at end of quarter	$94,426	$95,162	$95,484	$93,994

Derived "Annual rate of
  profit on stockholders'
  equity end of period"
	10.47%	21.29%	7.40%	11.33%

NOTE: The same approach is used in calculating the above annual earnings and dividing by the amount of *total assets* to produce the "annual rate of profit on total assets" as shown on all income statements in the QFR.

As long as Americans continue to celebrate the Thanksgiving and Christmas holiday season, the fourth quarter's earnings (over 40%) in the retail trade will always be much higher than in the other three quarters of the year. The retail industries' "annual rate of profit on stockholders' equity" of 21.29% at the end of the fourth quarter can never be achieved on an annual basis. If a figure of an annual rate is impossible of achievement, isn't its use misleading, regardless of the basis upon which it is derived?

In the lexicon of Wall Street, what the QFR is doing in its derivation of the "annual rate" is in fact "annualizing" the profits. "Annualizing" profits is the act of projecting the profits earned in a certain time period by multiplying them by what the multiple of the time period is to a year. An "annualized rate" has a distinctively different meaning than an "annual rate."

Furthermore, the "annual rates" used in the QFR refer to industry-wide and industry groups summary rates, which represent the consolidated rates of many corporations. Stockholders cannot purchase stock *in an industry* or *industry group* (they do not issue stock), or buy stock of all companies in an industry or industry group. Yet, the quotation excerpted from the Introduction of QFR states:

1. Annual Rate of Profit on Stockholders' Equity at End of Period . . . It measures *the rate of return which accrues to stockholders on their investment*. [Italics supplied.]

The above statement is categorically false. Therefore, much, if not all of Table 4-5 can be misleading.

Table 4-3 Income Statement
(Excerpt from Table 47.0 of QFR and used with permission)

All Retail Trade [2]

(million dollars)

	3Q 1986	4Q 1986	1Q 1987	2Q 1987	3Q [3] 1987
Net sales, receipts and operating revenues	122,305	140,833	120,804	127,408	
Less: Depreciation, depletion and amortization of property, plant and equipment	2,306	2,312	2,365	2,421	
Less: All other operating costs and expenses, including costs of good sold and selling, general, and administrative expenses	114,547	129,128	114,198	119,827	
Income (or loss) from operations	5,453	9,392	4,241	5,160	
Net non-operating income (expense)	-1,087	-488	-1,110	-689	
Income (or loss) before income taxes	4,365	8,905	3,131	4,471	
Less: Provision for current and deferred domestic income taxes	1,894	3,840	1,365	1,808	
Income (or loss) after income taxes	2,471	5,064	1,766	2,662	
Cash dividends charged to retained earnings in current quarter	832	919	818	1,000	
Net income retained in business	1,639	4,146	948	1,662	
Retained earnings at beginning of quarter	66,494	66,545	68,363	66,286	
Other direct credits (or charges) to retained earnings (net), including stock and other non-cash dividends, etc.	363	-852	-665	-411	
Retained earnings at end of quarter	68,496	69,839	68,645	67,538	

(percent of net sales)

INCOME STATEMENT IN RATIO FORMAT

Net sales, receipts, and operating revenues	100.0	100.0	100.0	100.0
Less: Depreciation, depletion, and amortization of property, plant and equipment	1.9	1.6	2.0	1.9
Less: All other operating costs and expenses	93.7	91.7	94.5	94.0
Income (or loss) from operations	4.5	6.7	3.5	4.0
Non-operating income (expense)	-0.9	-0.3	-0.9	-0.5
Income (or loss) before income taxes	3.6	6.3	2.6	3.5
Less: Provision for current and deferred domestic income taxes	1.5	2.7	1.1	1.4
Income (or loss) after income taxes	2.0	3.6	1.5	2.1

(percent)

OPERATING RATIOS
(see explanatory notes)

Annual rate of profit on stockholders' equity at end of period:				
Before income taxes	18.49	37.43	13.12	19.03
After taxes	10.47	21.29	7.40	11.33
Annual rate of profit on total assets:				
Before income taxes	6.97	14.51	4.95	7.10
After taxes	3.94	8.25	2.79	4.23

BALANCE SHEET RATIOS
(based on succeeding table)

Total current assets to total current liabilities	1.65	1.73	1.75	1.71
Total cash, U.S. Government and other securities to total current liabilities	0.15	0.18	0.16	0.17
Total stockholders' equity to total debt	1.25	1.32	1.22	1.18

[1]This asset size cutoff can lead to inconsistencies when comparing data on a quarter-to-quarter basis. Corporations that have exceeded the asset cutoff limit for the first time in the current quarter are not represented in previous quarter's data, and those falling below the cutoff are no longer represented.

[2]In the first quarter 1987, a number of corporations were reclassified by industry. To provide comparability, the four quarters of 1986 have been restated to reflect these reclassifications.

[3]See Publication Schedule, page XI. Third quarter estimates for Retail Trade will be published in the fourth quarter publication.

Table 4-4 Balance Sheet
(Excerpt from Table 47.1 of QFR, used with permission)

All Retail Trade[2]

	3Q 1986	4Q 1986	1Q 1987	2Q 1987	3Q[3] 1987
	(million dollars)				
ASSETS					
Cash and demand deposits in the U.S.	5,287	6,216	5,755	5,978	
Time deposits in the U.S., including negotiable certificates of deposit	1,615	1,536	1,562	1,823	
Total cash on hand and in U.S. banks	6,902	7,752	7,317	7,801	
Other short-term financial investments, including marketable and government securities, commercial paper, etc.	4,407	4,751	3,883	4,217	
Total cash, U.S. Government and other securities	11,309	12,503	11,200	12,018	
Trade accounts and trade notes receivable (less allowances for doubtful receivables)	36,253	37,305	36,971	35,230	
Inventories	74,721	65,508	69,727	70,108	
All other current assets	6,159	5,646	5,863	5,890	
Total current assets	128,441	120,963	123,761	123,247	
Depreciable and amortizable fixed assets, including construction in progress	121,580	121,963	124,511	124,449	
Land and mineral rights	9,541	9,696	9,845	9,799	
Less: Accumulated depreciation, depletion, and amortization	43,019	42,258	42,952	43,921	
Net property, plant, and equipment	88,102	89,401	91,404	90,327	
All other non-current assets, including investment in non-consolidated entities, long-term investments, intangibles, etc.	34,103	35,055	37,598	38,435	
Total Assets	250,646	245,419	252,762	252,009	
LIABILITIES AND STOCKHOLDERS'S EQUITY					
Short-term debt, original maturity of 1 year or less:					
a. Loans from banks	5,572	3,465	4,212	4,903	

b. Other short-term debt including commercial paper	6,636	3,762	4,313	5,792
Trade accounts and trade notes payable	36,668	32,792	33,213	33,261
Income taxes accrued, prior and current years, net of payments	5,272	6,053	4,372	3,698
Installments, due in 1 year or less, on long-term debt:				
a. Loans from banks	1,215	1,217	1,454	2,046
b. Other long-term debt	2,298	2,326	2,371	1,951
All other current liabilities, including excise and sales taxes, and accrued expenses	20,238	20,220	20,668	20,400
Total current liabilities	77,899	69,835	70,603	72,051
Long-term debt (due in more than 1 year):				
a. Loans from banks	14,793	14,877	15,184	14,786
b. Other long-term debt	45,216	46,224	50,791	50,464
All other non-current liabilities, including deferred income taxes, capitalized leases, and minority stockholders' interest in consolidated, domestic corporations	18,312	19,322	20,701	20,713
Total Liabilities	156,220	150,257	157,279	158,015
Capital stock and other capital (less treasury stock)	25,930	25,322	26,838	26,456
Retained earnings	68,496	69,839	68,645	67,538
Stockholders' Equity	94,426	95,162	95,484	93,994
Total Liabilities and Stockholders' Equity	250,646	245,419	252,762	252,009
NET WORKING CAPITAL				
Excess of total current assets over total current liabilities	50,543	51,128	53,157	51,196

SELECTED BALANCE SHEET RATIOS

	(percent of total assets)			
Total cash, U.S. Government and other securities	4.5	5.1	4.4	4.8
Trade accounts and trade notes receivable	14.5	15.2	14.6	14.0
Inventories	29.8	26.7	27.6	27.8
Total current assets	51.2	49.3	49.0	48.9
Net property, plant and equipment	35.1	36.4	36.2	35.8
Short-term debt including installments on long-term debt	6.2	4.3	4.9	5.8
Total current liabilities	31.1	28.5	27.9	28.6
Long-term debt	23.9	24.9	26.1	25.9
Total liabilities	62.3	61.2	62.2	62.7
Stockholders' equity	37.7	38.8	37.8	37.3

[1]This asset size cutoff can lead to inconsistencies when comparing data on a quarter-to-quarter basis. Corporations that have exceeded the asset cutoff limit for the first time in the current quarter are not represented in previous quarter's data, and those falling below the cutoff are no longer represented.

[2]In the first quarter 1987, a number of corporations were reclassified by industry. To provide comparability, the four quarters of 1986 have been restated to reflect these reclassifications.

[3]See Publication Schedule, page XI. Third quarter estimates for Retail Trade will be published in the fourth quarter publication.

Table 4-5 Annual Rates of Profit on
Stockholder's Equity by Division and Major Group
(Excerpt from Table D of QFR, used with permission)

Industry	Income before income taxes[1][2]					Income after income taxes[2]				
	3Q 1986	4Q 1986	1Q 1987	2Q 1987	3Q 1987	3Q 1986	4Q 1986	1Q 1987	2Q 1987	3Q 1987
All manufacturing corporations	13.9	13.2	16.9	21.1	21.5	8.4	8.5	10.8	14.0	14.5
Nondurable manufacturing corporations	17.4	17.0	18.7	22.2	24.6	10.7	11.1	12.5	14.8	16.3
Food and kindred products	24.6	31.5	21.6	27.7	26.0	15.5	20.0	13.6	17.2	16.9
Tobacco manufactures	NA	NA	NA	NA	NA	NA	NA	NA	NA	NA
Textile mill products	24.1	27.4	20.8	20.5	26.1	13.0	15.9	12.0	11.9	17.4
Paper and allied products	16.7	20.8	20.6	24.3	26.9	10.6	12.3	12.4	14.7	16.9
Printing and publishing	35.0	33.6	21.5	28.9	32.2	20.2	20.7	12.5	16.9	19.7
Chemicals and allied products	24.0	13.8	25.2	22.0	31.7	15.3	8.5	16.6	14.7	20.7
Industrial chemicals and synthetics	18.0	10.3	21.7	24.7	37.2	11.9	5.3	14.3	16.1	22.8
Drugs	38.4	37.3	34.8	28.9	31.0	24.2	28.0	24.4	20.4	21.6
Petroleum and coal products	1.6	3.7	9.5	16.3	14.8	1.0	4.3	7.9	12.9	10.6
Rubber and miscellaneous plastics products	29.7	13.8	28.3	34.5	30.8	18.7	6.7	20.3	24.6	20.8
Other nondurable manufacturing corporations	17.8	27.5	21.0	10.1	25.8	9.1	17.5	13.0	3.8	17.7
Durable manufacturing corporations	10.4	9.4	15.1	20.1	18.2	6.0	5.9	9.2	13.3	12.8
Stone, clay and glass products	20.0	22.8	20.2	28.4	29.1	12.5	12.7	13.4	18.6	20.0
Primary metal industries	-28.1	-2.0	14.5	13.7	19.8	-30.7	-4.7	10.0	6.9	13.3
Iron and steel	-103.7	-20.1	24.0	28.7	24.0	-108.9	-25.2	18.5	18.5	16.5
Nonferrous metals	5.1	5.7	10.3	6.5	17.8	3.7	4.1	6.3	1.4	11.8
Fabricated metal products	14.4	12.2	11.9	21.9	21.9	7.5	6.5	5.7	13.7	15.2
Machinery, except electrical	8.9	8.1	6.5	16.2	14.8	5.8	5.1	2.8	11.5	10.2
Electrical and electronic equipment	11.5	11.0	14.6	16.3	16.6	7.1	9.1	9.1	10.7	11.0
Transportation equipment	13.0	9.9	23.9	25.8	16.3	9.6	7.5	15.9	17.8	12.9
Motor vehicles and equipment	10.2	13.0	26.9	29.2	13.6	8.5	11.9	18.5	20.5	12.2
Aircraft, guided missiles and parts	18.0	4.1	20.0	20.1	21.2	11.8	-0.9	12.6	13.3	14.1
Instruments and related products	16.2	-3.2	16.9	17.4	19.8	11.0	-5.4	11.1	11.5	13.6
Other durable manufacturing corporations	20.5	20.3	17.0	28.5	28.5	12.3	12.0	9.3	17.3	18.3
All mining corporations	-15.5	-18.4	-3.6	-4.0	2.1	-14.7	-16.8	-5.0	-7.0	-0.3
All retail trade corporations	18.5	37.4	13.1	19.0	NA	10.5	21.3	7.4	11.3	NA
All wholesale trade corporations	13.5	18.5	14.3	13.7	17.1	7.0	10.1	9.0	7.9	10.7

All of the above discussion of QFR's "annual rate of profit on stockholders' equity at end of period" is superimposed upon the reservations expressed earlier concerning the term "percent return on equity."

Trading Strategies

MOST OF THE PRESENTATIONS HEREIN ARE DIRECTED TOWARD STOCK market investing. However, in any massive group of people we find many of different persuasions. Some are of one political party or another; some are optimists, others pessimists; some are extroverts, other introverts; some are strong, some not; some are educated, some aren't; some are lucky, others are not, and not wanting to beat a dead dog, I'll end this parlance with: some are investors and some are stock traders.

Many traders in stocks are referred to as "day traders." Their mode of activity is far different from the usual investor. Usual investors buy stocks and hold them for indefinite periods; sometimes for months, sometimes for years. They are contrasted with day traders who daily sit in stock broker boardrooms watching the stock ticker crawl or computer monitors flash every change in price of stocks.

Day traders possess up-to-the-minute knowledge of stock prices, volume, and so forth when they enter trades (either on the long or short side) and usually close them out before the day's end. Some traders effect a number of trades during the day, particularly when trading: 1. index options such as the S&P 500 and 100, the Major Market Index, or Value Line Index; and 2. futures contracts covering numerous commodities. (Chapter 6 is devoted to stock options and chapter 7 to futures contracts.)

Several trading considerations for stock *traders only* are offered in the following pages.

STOP-LOSS ORDERS

Some investors, after having been in the market for some time, may feel they have enough expertise to employ what they look upon as sophisticated techniques, such as the stop-loss order. This practice, however, can prove to be a double-edged sword.

A *stop-loss order* is one that calls for selling a stock at a price usually a few points below or above its current market price. A stop-loss order is often placed at the time a stock is bought, but can be made at any time of ownership.

The buyer of 100 shares of Company A's stock at $50 per share places an immediate stop-loss order at $47. He reasons that if the stock rises substantially (after all, it was as high as $74 this very year), he will share in the gain, but if it should fall, all he can lose is three points plus commission at both ends of the trade. This thinking can prove to be self-deluding.

Two unexpected hazards may face the stop-loss participant. First, he could be "whipsawed." The stock could fall to the stop-loss price, and then, presto, the stock may immediately turn around and make significant gains. Second, he could become the victim of a snowballing effect on the downside. When advance orders are placed in a specialist's book to sell a stock at a certain price, and the specialist knows there are many more stop-loss orders at that level and at various lower levels, with few buy orders at such points, he may very well allow the public to decide the level at which the price should fall.

When our investor friend placed his stop-loss order for Company A at $47, there was no guarantee made by anyone that his stock would or could be sold at that precise price. All that is required of the broker once the stock has made a single sale at $47 is to sell the stock at the next bid price. If that price should be $46 or $45, then our investor will suffer a $400 or $500 loss plus commissions, instead of the $300 he had believed.

Our friend, however, in spite of his added experience, is indefatigable. Such a fluke couldn't happen again. So he watches the market gyrations of Company A. Finally, after exercising the greatest of patience in not jumping in on the buy side, the stock once again turns and drops. . . . He waits and waits . . . finally it hits a low of 30! He hurriedly calls his broker and, attempting to conceal his inner excitement and after asking the broker's advice (merely as a polite gesture, for he had no intention of following it if it even hinted at an opposite view), he orders 100 shares at the market price. The purchase was made at $30\frac{1}{4}$, and thereafter, the stock rose to $37. Great! Our friend, however, held—after all, the stock is still only half of what it hit this year! Shortly afterward, the pendulum started another downward swing. When the stock reached $32 our friend placed a stop-loss order at $29. The stock was sold at $28\frac{1}{2}$. Our investor is now even more experienced.

In spite of any admonition against placing stop-loss orders, many investors will continue such practice. A final word of caution to them is to *remember the order*. Stop-loss orders are generally good until cancelled. Sometimes they may remain open for a period of months. At times, investors switch from one broker to another, and some may have more than one broker. Almost every experienced broker can recall one or more situations where an old stop-loss order is executed—much to the dismay of the investor, who, having forgotten the order, had previously sold the stock. So, unless an investor can afford the possibility of unexpectedly finding himself "going short" in a stock, he should remember the open-ended stop-loss orders.

THE ARMS INDEX—A Short Term Trading Index

After many years of usage, the term *Trin* was changed to *Arms* to give recognition to its originator's name, Richard W. Arms, Jr.

Arms is amongst the stock market symbols reported continuously each trading day on FNN's Cable T.V. System and on many quotation devices. It represents a short-term trading index which, as its composition changes, is designed to reflect whether the market will continue in its up and down mode or reverse the trend.

Its formula is:

1. Divide the number of stocks that are advancing in price by the number declining in price.

2. Divide the volume of shares advancing by the volume declining.

3. Divide 1. by 2.

Example:

$\dfrac{500 \quad \text{Stocks advancing in price}}{400 \quad \text{Stocks declining in price}}$	
$\dfrac{30M \quad \text{Advancing volume of shares}}{45M \quad \text{Declining volume of shares}}$	$= \dfrac{1.25}{.67} = 1.87 \text{ Bearish}$

For short term trading, a result of 1.00 or more is considered bearish, and .99 or less is considered bullish.

Over time, little in Wall Street remains constant. Occasionally, just when you feel centered upon a successful plan, approach, or technique, something comes along that diminishes or even demolishes its effectiveness.

Such an example of one of many influences that constitute a "Wall Street Challenge" involves "dividend capture trades," and its effect on the validity of the Trin Index.

DAY OF THE WEEK EFFECT

Any number of stock traders are continually on the alert to identify some strategy they can latch onto, if only for a short period of time. They know from experience that no scheme lasts forever, and they are wise enough to change a strategy as soon as possible after it ceases to perform as expected. Then they search out another and test it for a judgmental period before putting it to use.

One short-term strategy is referred to as the "day of the week effect." A short-term trading period in the Dow Industrials is shown in Table 5-1. The table covers a 21-week span of trading in the Dow Industrials. The year of 1987 ended with the Dow at 1938.83. Twenty-one weeks later on May 27, 1988, the Dow closed at 1956.44, representing a change of plus 17.61 points in 21 weeks! Yet, some things happened on the way to "nowhere."

During the twenty-one weeks:

1. On the 20 Mondays the Dow rose 12 times and dropped 8 for a net gain on Mondays of 221.13 points.

2. On the 21 Tuesdays the Dow rose 12 times and dropped 9 for a net gain on Tuesdays of 85.71 points.

3. On the 20 Fridays the Dow rose 12 times and dropped 8 for a net gain on Fridays of 2.33 points.

4. On the 21 Wednesdays the Dow rose 8 times and dropped 13 for a net loss of 102.97 points.

5. On the 21 Thursdays the Dow rose 10 times and dropped 11 for a net loss of 188.59 points.

Based upon the above record, some consideration could have been given to bullish trades with a market close order on Friday afternoons for the action on Mondays and to bearish trades with a market close order on Tuesday afternoons for the action on Wednesdays and

Table 5-1 The Dow—Five Months Ended May 27th, 1988

Week	Monday Up	Monday Down	Tuesday Up	Tuesday Down	Wednesday Up	Wednesday Down	Thursday Up	Thursday Down	Friday Up	Friday Down	Week Up	Week Down
1/ 3/88	76.42		16.25		6.30		14.09			140.58		27.52
15	33.82			16.58		3.82		8.62	39.96		44.76	
22	7.79			27.52		57.20	.17		24.20			52.56
29	42.95			25.86		9.45	18.90		28.18		54.71	
	160.97	-0-	16.25	69.96	6.30	70.47	33.16	8.62	92.34	140.58	99.47	80.08
2/ 5/88		13.59	8.29			28.35		1.00		13.09		47.74
12		14.76	18.74		47.58			.50	21.72		72.78	
19	Holiday		22.71			4.98		14.58	28.18		31.33	
26	25.70			1.17	.83			22.38	5.64		8.62	
	25.70	28.35	49.74	1.17	48.41	33.33	-0-	38.46	55.54	13.09	112.73	47.74
3/ 4/88	48.41			1.16	.83			7.80		5.63	34.65	
11		1.49	24.70			6.80		48.24	8.95			22.88
18	15.09			2.66	16.91		21.72		1.33		52.39	
25		20.23		.99	1.49			43.77		44.92		108.42
	63.50	21.72	24.70	4.81	19.23	6.80	21.72	99.81	10.28	50.55	87.04	131.30

Continued

Table 5-1 Continued

Week	Monday Up	Monday Down	Tuesday Up	Tuesday Down	Wednesday Up	Wednesday Down	Thursday Up	Thursday Down	Friday Up	Friday Down	Week Up	Week Down
4/ 1/88	.82		18.57			20.22	9.94		Holiday		9.11	
8		7.46	16.91		64.16		.50		28.02		102.13	
15	5.80		14.09			2.98		101.46	8.29			76.26
22		5.81		8.62		14.09	1.99		27.69		1.16	
29	20.88		8.79		3.15			6.63		8.95	17.24	
	27.50	13.27	58.36	8.62	67.31	37.29	12.43	108.09	64.00	8.95	129.64	76.26
5/ 6/88	10.94		15.09			22.05		16.08		12.77		24.87
13		10.11	6.30			37.80	2.15		22.55			16.91
20	17.08	11.11	21.05	21.22		35.32	7.63			6.13		37.96
27	28.02	21.22	42.44		-0-	1.16	5.38			10.31	3.85	79.74
Total	305.69	84.56	191.49	105.78	141.25	244.22	82.47	271.06	244.71	242.38	432.73	415.12
	84.56		105.78			141.25		82.47	242.38		415.12	
Net	221.13		85.71		102.97		188.59		2.33		17.61	
Number of days	12	8	12	9	8	13	10	11	12	8		

Thursdays. Exceptions would have existed whenever the Dow went up over a point on four consecutive Mondays. Whenever four winning trades in a row occur, it would seem prudent to sit back and wait for the winning streak to be broken before resuming the trades.

Caution: The above is based upon only a five-month trailing period. No stock market trading strategy should be set in concrete. With the stock market being fluid, the above data must change again and again. While, currently, Mondays and Tuesdays have been the leading Dow up days, and Wednesdays and Thursdays are the leading down days, they all could switch to other days.

It is good to remember that whenever someone comes up with a plan that seems to be a world-beater, somewhere, somehow, something happens that negates the whole scheme. Many strategies have proven successful for a time, only to fizzle out some time down the road. The same will happen to the above. Otherwise there would be no horse racing, stock market, or casinos.

Yet, during time spans in which a trading mode points up a fairly consistent pattern, strategies could be considered by a nimble trader that could prove lucrative. The key discipline is to be flexible: Stick with a plan while it is successful; when it starts to fail, stop and wait for a new pattern to assert itself. The changes in trading modes can be identified if a person maintains his own record showing the daily and weekly movements in the Dow.

6

Trading in Stock Options

STOCK OPTIONS MIGHT BE CONSIDERED SECOND COUSINS TO FUTURES contracts.

Futures contracts were preceded by forward contracts, which served a national purpose and interest. However, only some *futures* contracts serve such a purpose and interest. (See also chapter 7.)

Engaging in trading options such as *puts* can serve as an "insurance policy" against a bad drop in the prices of stocks held by an individual, fund, and so on, because when puts are bought and, subsequently, the prices of the underlying stocks fall, the value of the puts increases, thus offsetting, in part at least, the paper losses in the stocks. By and large, however, when an individual buys and sells puts and calls he is engaging in gambling, not investing.

OPTION TERMINOLOGY

Before becoming immersed in the subject of options, you must first became familiar with the terminology relative to puts and calls. Some of this terminology is used in Table 6-1. Following are some common terms and their definitions.

A call option A *call* gives the buyer an option, but not an obligation, to buy 100 shares of stock (or other instrument) at a fixed price for a specified period of time.

121

Table 6-1 Options Terminology

	Expiration Month	Strike Price	Market Price of Underlying Security	Market Price of Option	Intrinsic Value	Premium	Option Condition
Examples:							
Call A	Feb.	$ 80	$ 84	$ 9	$ 4	$ 5	In the money
Call B	Feb.	70	70	5	0	5	At the money
Call C	Feb.	100	98	4	0	6	Out of the money
Put D	Feb.	70	65	8	5	3	In the money
Put E	Feb.	60	60	3	0	3	At the money
Put F	Feb.	80	83	4	0	7	Out of the money

A put option   A *put* is the opposite of a call. It gives the buyer a right, but not an obligation, to sell 100 shares of the underlying security, etc., at a fixed price within a specified time.

Strike price   The *strike* or "exercise" price is the dollar amount at which a holder of a call can purchase the security or a holder of a put may sell the security within the stated period of time.

In the money   A call option is *in the money* when the market price of the underlying security is higher than the strike price. A put option is *in the money* when the market price of the underlying security is less than the strike price.

At the money   An option (put or call) is *at the money* when the current market price of the underlying security is the same as the strike price.

Out of the money   A call option is *out of the money* when the market price of the underlying security is less than the strike price. A put option is *out of the money* when the price of the underlying security is greater than the strike price.

Intrinsic value   The *intrinsic value of a call* represents the excess of the dollar amount of the market price of the underlying security over the strike price. The *intrinsic value of a put* represents the excess of the dollar amount of the strike price over the market price of the underling security.

Premium   The premium of an in the money call represents the excess of the market price of the underlying security over the strike price, deducted from the market price of the option.

The premium of an at the money call represents the market price of the option.

The premium of an out of the money call represents the excess of the strike price over the market price of the underlying security, plus the market price of the option.

The premium of an in the money put represents the excess of the strike price over the market price of the underlying security, deducted from the market price of the option.

The premium of an at the money put represents the amount of the market price of the option.

The premium of an out of the money put represents the excess of the market value of the underlying security over the strike price plus the market price of the option.

Expiration date   Options generally expire on the Saturday following the third Friday in an expiration month, after which the options no
longer exist.

RISK

The risk to the buyer of an option is limited to its purchase price, plus
the broker's commission. All call buyers must be bullish because they
can only make money on the call if the underlying security rises in
price. Also, it must be realized that a call is a wasting asset that will, at
expiration time, become worthless if the price of the underlying security is at or below the strike price. Puts will also become worthless if,
at expiration time, the price of the underlying security is at or above
the strike price.

WRITING CALL OPTIONS

The writing of a covered call option is one of two ways calls are made
available for purchase. The second is referred to as a "naked option,"
which means the sale of the call is unhedged. The writing of a covered
call represents the hedging of a position. An investor may be in doubt
about a stock he owns, yet he wishes to retain it. He may decide to
write (sell) a covered call option. If his underlying stock falls below the
strike price at expiration, he will retain the stock and the price
received for the option. This minimizes the paper loss in his security.
However, if the underlying stock rises in price above the strike price,
the call can be exercised at any time by its buyer. The owner of the
security must then sell the stock to the buyer at the strike price. The
writer of the call retains the price paid for the option and any dividends
that may have been paid on the stock. In the event the buyer of the call
exercises the call prior to an ex-dividend date, he is entitled to the dividend, even though he may not as yet have received the stock certifi-
cate which is "in transfer."

The writing of covered calls is considered a conservative strategy
for investors in stocks.

WRITING NAKED OPTIONS

When a put or call is sold without owning the underlying security, it
represents a greater risk than when writing *covered options*. When
writing (selling) naked options there is a potential unlimited risk on the
call in a rising market and on the put in a falling market, while the
return is limited to the market prices received for the options when
sold. The amount of the losses, however, can be truncated by buying
back the options at any time prior to their expiration.

OTHER STRATEGIES

Other strategies that are practiced by some option traders involve buying and selling combinations of options simultaneously. These involve such terms as *spreads* and *straddles*. When the investor employs the use of such strategies, he or she is doubling the risk because of a possible loss on both sides of the transactions.

As an example, the writer of a straddle (representing a put and call on a specific underlying security and at the same strike price) will receive the market price of both options. His risk, however, potentially has no limit; in the event the market price of the underlying security falls below the strike price in excess of the combined market prices received for the options, or if the market price of the security rises above the combined prices received, the writer would sustain a loss when one or the other is exercised. If both are exercised, his or her losses could double.

Always remember to consider the risks before engaging in esoteric strategies.

PREMIUMS ON CALLS AND PUTS

Of the two elements of the cost of options, i.e., the intrinsic value, if any, and the "time" value, the most important to consider is the latter.

Very often the time value of an option is so excessive in price, it, alone, might militate against its purchase. One way to determine whether such value is too high is to consider it "interest" being paid for the option and equate it with what such interest would be on an annual basis.

For example:

At the close of business on August 19, 1988 the IBM Sept. 110 call sold for $5^1/8$. The market price of the stock closed at $112^1/2$. The intrinsic value of the call was $2^1/2$, and the time value, of less than four weeks to expiration on September 16, was $2^5/8$. The interest equivalent of $2^5/8$ on the market value of $112^1/2$ amounts to 2.33% for a four-week period.

The annualized equivalent percentage interest of such a call is shown below:

$$2.33\% \times \frac{52}{4} = 30.29\%$$

Should any investor pay such an annualized rate of interest to purchase *any* kind of investment instrument?

It is important to remember the component considerations that affect the pricing of options:

- The time span before an option expires affects its price. A longer time span adds more to its price than a shorter time span.

- The volatility of an underlying stock influences the pricing of its options. A high beta stock adds more to the pricing of an option than a low beta one. That is because an out of the money put or call on a high beta stock can more readily become in the money; one in the money can substantially increase in value commensurate with moves in the underlying stock.

- The price of the underlying stock has an influence on the pricing of an option on that stock. The higher the price of a stock, the higher would be its usual effect on the pricing of the option. This is because a higher priced stock generally moves, whether up or down, a larger number of points than a low-priced stock, and their options are likely to be affected by such moves.

- Lastly, current interest rates on borrowings to maintain position of options held by market makers are passed on in the price of premiums paid by buyers and sellers of puts and calls.

POINT GAINS VS. PERCENTAGES—
When Buying Puts and Calls

Oftentimes the success of a trade in a stock is measured by the percentage gain achieved by the investor. For example, if an investor bought 100 shares of stock at $20 a share and it rose $2, it would represent a gain of $200 or 10%. (Commissions not considered.)

With respect to a purchased call or put, success is measured by the number of points the call increases or the put drops, respectively, at the time the trade is closed. In addition, success can be magnified because of leverage inherent in options. With an option the cost may be 10% or less than the cost of 100 shares of the underlying stock. Yet, when a call increases in price to an extent that the time value portion of the premium has been absorbed, then the full excess of the market price of the stock over the strike price represents 100% intrinsic value; for each additional $1 increase in the market price of the stock, the call should increase dollar for dollar.

Again, remember that *higher-priced stocks move a greater number of points both up and down than lower-priced stocks*, even though the percentage move can be the same. For example: A $20 stock rises $2 for a 10% gain while an $80 stock rises $8 for a 10% gain. This points to the general advantage (if one engages in buying puts and calls) in buying puts and calls of underlying relatively higher-priced stocks.

Warning: If the trade proves to be a losing one, the premium lost will be somewhat more than would have been a premium on a low-priced underlying stock; however, if the trade is successful, the chances are the gain will be much greater.

Refer to Table 6-2 on p. 128 some specific real-life examples.

BUYING PUTS AND CALLS

Now let's consider the matter of gambling in the stock market. It is assumed you have experience in the market, that you are very knowledgeable, and that you understand all the strategies presented in the foregoing pages. So, why not then go for the big bucks through the leverage offered in options?

Even for those who are quite experienced, the premiums charged on index options, more often than not, are so high they are tough to beat. The premiums are based upon a value of the time remaining to exercise the option, the intrinsic value of the option, if any, and an estimate by the market makers in options of the direction of the market, interest rates, volatility, and so on.

When buying puts and calls, you are face-to-face with an opponent taking the position opposite to yours; in fact, he does this for a living. Because of the size of the premium, the advantage rests with him.

Some examples:

- If the market index or underlying stock remains about the same from the time of your purchase of the call or put, you will lose the amount equivalent to the premium, plus commission.

- If you buy a call on the S&P 500 or 100 index, then the market drops and you sell the call, you may lose the full value of the premium plus the commission in and out, or the equivalent of $100 for each $1 down-move in the index, up to but not exceeding the original cost of the option.

- If you buy a put on the S&P 500 or 100 index, then the market rises and you sell the put, you may lose the full value of the premium plus the commission in and out, or the equivalent of $100 for each $1 up-move in the index, up to but not exceeding the original cost of the option.

- If you purchase a put or call and the market moves in your favor, you can win some money.

Table 6-2 Percentage Gains

	At Close 4/1/88		At Close 4/8/88		Gain of Stock		Gain of Call	
	Stock Price	Call Price (May 17½)	Stock Price	Call Price (May 17½)	Amount	%	Amount	%
The Limited	19½	2¾ April 100	20½	3½ April 100	$1.00	5.0	$ 75.00	27.3
I.B.M.	107⅝	8⅛	111⅝	12¼ April 100	4.00	4.1	412.50	283.7
		Percent cost of IBM call over the limited call					Percent gain of IBM call over the limited call	
		195%					450%	
First Chicago Corp.	23¾	July 22½ 2½ April 155	25¼	July 22½ 3½ April 155	$1.50	6.3	$100.00	40.0
Merck	157.00	4½	164⅞	10 April 155	7.87	5.0	$550.00	122.2
		Percent cost of Merck call over First Chicago call					Percent gain of Merck call over First Chicago call	
		80%					450%	

Caveat: Looking back at historical performance is infinitely more simple than prospective successful actions. See later comment for percent of losers when buying puts and calls.

NOTE: the SP 100 Index (OEX) moves up or down about a point with about every 8-point move in the Dow Industrials. The Major Market Index (XMI) moves up or down about a point with about every 5 point move in the Dow Industrials.

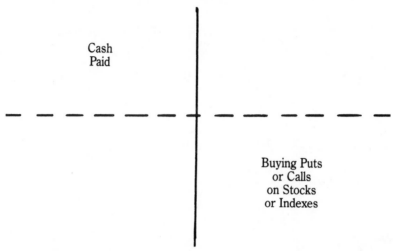

Cash
Paid

Buying Puts
or Calls
on Stocks
or Indexes

Fig. 6-1. Estimated Negative Factor: Over 60% of individuals who buy puts or calls lose money!

Psychologically, the vanishing time span remaining in which to exercise the closing of an option hangs like the Sword of Damocles over your head. As time passes, you eventually know you must get out of the option, perhaps with a profit or a loss, within, say, a week. As the pressure builds up, you finally take action, and the timing of the sell action can be far more crucial than the timing of when to buy. To wit:

Always remember that regardless of one's expertise, the market can show no mercy. Its alacrity in causing deep-felt humility even amongst Wall Street's gurus has been apparent again and again. One time, when I believed the stock market was ripe for a significant drop, I purchased puts (using risk funds only) in Westinghouse Electric and NCR. A month and a half later the puts were sold with a profit of 29% and 20%—a fine return in a period of only 1¹/₂ months, right? Read on:

Three working days later on October 19, 1987, the puts could have been sold at a profit of 355% and 261%.

Please permit me a final word: Never lament a closed trade; it is over the dam. If you feel like crying all the way to the bank, try thinking only of the success you've achieved.

7

Trading in Commodities

FORWARD CONTRACTS BEGAN IN THE UNITED STATES AS A RESULT OF weather or other economic factors that impacted the price farmers and ranchers were able to receive for their products.

To ensure that they could remain in business in the event prices for their products dropped significantly at harvest time or when brought to market, many farmers and ranchers availed themselves of the use of forward contracts, one-on-one with the buyers, that stipulated they deliver at least part of their production at a specified time and price.

Forward contracts were also beneficial to the users of the products. Businesspersons then and now must be able to plan their costs of production well in advance. Forward contracts ensured delivery of source materials at a predetermined price.

Like forward contracts, the current futures contracts also benefit the consuming public by helping to ensure a continuing flow of products and a reign on prices, thus serving a national interest and benefit.

Assume that cocoa beans are selling currently at $1200 a metric ton, and in a short period of time the price rises to $2000 a ton. Wouldn't it be wise for Hershey Foods Corporation (which cannot make chocolate without cocoa beans) to engage in futures contracts in order to prevent a substantial increase in price of all their products at a later date? Wouldn't the same apply to the future price of hogs for a company like Oscar Mayer who makes hot dogs?

Forward contracts changed to futures contracts when the various Commodity Exchanges were established. Under their aegis the offer of commodities are sold to the dealers at the Exchanges. Purchases are also made through the dealers. The one-on-one relationship today rarely, if ever, exists.

The Commodity Exchanges assume responsibility for the eventual execution of the contracts, ensuring quantity and quality.

Today, a few of the new commodity futures may also, at least indirectly, serve the national interest and benefit. One applies to the businessperson or corporation who sells products internationally. Such a person knows the sales price he or she must obtain for the products to turn a profit. It may prove prudent to avoid, through currency futures contracts, the fluctuations in the value of foreign currencies in relation to the dollar. These could have an adverse affect on the businessperson's ability to compete and on profits, which, in chain reaction, could affect prices ultimately paid for products sold in the United States.

Today, many futures contracts when compared with investing in stocks and bonds, represent gambling vehicles for speculators. The investor in equities or bonds can expect to receive some kind of return in dividends or interest, plus a possibility of a capital gain (or loss), when selling the instrument. In futures trading the speculator knows the result of a trade is limited to a capital gain or loss. Therefore, the speculator's consideration should boil down to simply: What must be done to help produce net dollar gains even when the number of losing trades exceeds the number of profitable ones?

To encourage successful futures trading, the trader can employ fundamental and technical analysis, in much the same manner as an astute investor in the stock market.

Actually there are a few factors that affect both the stock market and the futures markets. Interest rates can certainly play an important part in commodity trading and the stock market, and so can inflation. However, aside from these, most others are unique to either stocks or commodities.

Different categories of futures, for instance, often react to news regarding the specific commodity: news of bumper crops or crop damage, number of heads of cattle in feedlots, action of the oil cartel, and news of oil spills. All of these factors can affect supply and demand.

You can employ fundamental analysis by making use of raw data obtainable from a number of sources including:

- The Crop Reporting Board of the Department of Agriculture, which reports on conditions and estimates of production.

- The Weather Bureau, which issues reports during the summer months concerning rainfall in general areas for specific crops such as wheat and corn.

- The Federal Reserve, for news affecting the Federal Funds rate, which represents the rates of interest charged by banks for overnight loans to other banks, as well as for fluctuations in the discount rate, reserve requirement for banks, and the rate of broker's margin requirements. Each of these could have an impact on financial index futures, including the S&P 500 Index, the Major Market Index, (which closely resembles stocks in the Dow Jones Industrials), and the Value Line Composite Index.

- Many brokerage firms, which have "accredited" commodity brokers issue (some daily) releases on commodities, together with their trading recommendations.

NOTE: The Commodity Futures Trading Commission controls all activities of the Commodity Trading Exchanges in the United States. The National Futures Association is responsible for: 1. Testing applicants for assurance of their knowledge of commodity trading; and 2. Checking the financial and credit standing of applicants prior to granting their accrediation as a community broker (akin to but different from a stock broker.)

CHARTING

The use of charting by technical analysts is considered extremely important in furnishing timing signals to determine when to enter and exit a futures contract.

In addition, fundamental factors can and do influence commodity prices, which are reflected in charts showing trends and changes in trends.

The chartist examines the charts and interprets the different resulting formations: rounding bottoms – bullish; down-gap openings – temporarily bearish; head and shoulders – bearish; reverse head and shoulders – bullish; up-gap openings – temporarily bullish; double tops – bearish; double bottoms – bullish; breaking resistance levels – bullish; trend lines with lower lows and lower highs – bearish; trend lines with higher lows and higher highs – bullish, and so on.

The viewing of charts by different individuals often results in differing interpretations, just like art enthusiasts interpreting abstract paintings. This is often a result of "subjective seeing," in that different people see what they subconsciously want to see. Others might recognize one aspect of a chart, giving it more importance over another. On the other hand, when a large number of futures traders view charts the same way within the same time span, and take action in accordance with their views, the market will react in concert, thus producing a self-induced effect of indeterminate duration.

While charting is a technical tool that can be effective, this book will emphasize the analysis of open interest.[1]

ANALYSIS OF OPEN INTEREST

Open interest represents the number of futures contracts of a specific commodity that have not as yet been liquidated by a close order or by delivery or receipt of the commodity.

There is widespread perception that when open interest increases, it means "fresh money" is being put in the commodity contract, with probabilities then favoring a continuation of an uptrend in price or perhaps a halting or turnaround of a downtrend. Is this a valid belief? Let's try to find the answers.

First we must learn what triggers an increase in or decrease of open interest:

1. Open interest increases by "one" through the purchase of a futures contract and also by "one" through initiation of a short sale of a futures contract.

2. At any given time, open interest represents futures contracts that have not been closed out or liquidated as yet by a subsequent sale of a long position, by subsequent purchase of a short position, by delivery, or by receipt for the commodity.

3. The following chart depicts how the number of open interest is affected by the transactions in steps 1 and 2 above:

Previous Open Interest	Affect on Open Interest Increase Decrease	Current Open Interest
4000		

A. The purchase of six long
   position contracts 6 4006

---

[1] Excellent Commodity Charts may be obtained from Commodity Research Bureau Futures Chart Services, 30 South Wacker Drive, Suite 1820 Chicago, Ill., 60606.

B. The closeout of nine long
   position contracts 9 3997

C. The initiation of five short
   position contracts . . . . 5 .4002

D. The closeout of four short
   position contracts 4 3998

E. Now let's visualize the effect
   of initiation of a large
   number of short positions as
   opposed to the initiation of
   long positions, all of which
   are still open:

   1. Initiation of short
      positions 2500 6498
   2. Initiation of long
      positions 300 6798

As far as I know, there is no public information available giving a breakout of open interest showing the number of unliquidated long positions and unliquidated short positions. However, with further analysis, based upon data that are available, we may find what impact changes in open interest may have on the price of the commodity. While doing so, we must also consider the supply and demand law of economics.

In and of itself, however, rising open interest does not always bring with it rising prices. If it did, wouldn't it be easier to "beat the commodity market?" The lack of published data mentioned above may prove a boon to those who acquire additional knowledge through further analysis. Read on.

On October 4, 1982 the spot price of silver was $8.39 an ounce, with the total open interest contracts numbering 12,082. During the next 20 weeks the spot price steadily increased to $14.57 on February 21, 1983, while the total open interest climbed to 40,261. In 18 of the 20 weeks the total open interest increased. In 15 weeks the spot price of silver increased. Overall, there was a steady increase in total open interest and a trend of higher prices, which is in accord with the common belief of what should happen.

But note what then happened! In the week of February 28, 1983 the total open interest was 41,647, an *increase* of 1,386 over the 40,261 of the previous week, and the spot price dropped from $14.57 to $12.57 for a loss of $2.00 an ounce. This represents a loss on a single long position of $10,000 in one week.

Reviewing the open interest increases and decreases chart below, we know when the number of new long positions plus the number of new short positions exceed the number of closed long positions plus the number of closed short positions, a net increase in open interest occurs. Then, according to economics, if the new long positions exceeded the new short positions, the price of the commodity should rise. However, during the week of February 28, 1983, the rise in open interest was accompanied by a very large decrease in price! Wouldn't the answer then be that such increase in open interest represented a preponderance of new short positions (reflecting selling) over new long positions (reflecting buying), with such net selling precipitating the decline in price during the week of February 28, 1983?

Let's review some recent action in the silver futures covering the period of February 27 through June 19, 1989.

Date	Price	Increase (Decrease)	Open Interest	(Decrease)
2/27/89	5.923		94,854	
3/ 6/89	5.801	(.122)	92,401	(2,453)(1)
3/13/89	6.068	.267	91,985	(416)(2)
3/20/89	6.124	.056	94,239	2,254 (3)
3/27/89	6.003	(.121)	96,004	1,765 (4)
4/ 3/89	5.778	(.227)	97,994	1,990 (4)
4/10/89	5.769	(.009)	97,791	(203)(1)
4/17/89	5.805	.036	100,209	2,418 (3)
4/24/89	5.756	(.049)	102,102	1,893 (4)
5/ 1/89	5.601	(.155)	100,821	(1,281)(1)
5/ 8/89	5.598	(.003)	91,085	(9,736)(1)
5/15/89	5.535	(.063)	92,415	1,330 (4)
5/22/89	5.229	(.306)	93,072	657 (4)
5/29/89	5.252	.023	87,647	(5,425)(2)
6/ 5/89	5.298	.046	86,125	(1,522)(2)
6/12/89	5.162	(.136)	87,137	1,012 (4)
6/19/89	5.285	.123	87,582	445 (3)

When studying the chart, note the following movements in open interest and commodity prices:

1. Open interest dropped and the price dropped. Doesn't this mean, economically, that there was more closeout of long positions plus closeout of short positions than the initiation of new long positions plus new short positions, and also that the closeout of long positions (requiring selling) exceeded the closeout of short positions (requiring purchasing)? These influences occurred in four of 16 weeks.

2. Open interest dropped and the price increased. Doesn't this mean, economically, that there was more closeout of short positions plus the closeout of long positions than the initiation of new long and new short positions, and also that the closeout of short positions (requiring purchasing) exceeded the number of closeout of long positions (requiring selling)? These influences occurred in three of 16 weeks.

3. Open interest increased and the price increased. Doesn't this mean, economically, that there was more initiation of new long positions plus initiation of new short positions than the closeout of long positions plus the closeout of short positions, and that the initiation of new long positions (requiring purchasing) exceeded the initiation of new short positions (requiring selling)? These influences occurred in three of 16 weeks.

4. Open interest increased and the price dropped. Doesn't this mean, economically, that there was more initiation of new long positions plus initiation of new short positions than the closeout of long positions plus the closeout of short positions, and that the initiation of new short positions (requiring selling) exceeded the initiation of new long positions (requiring purchasing)? These factors occurred in six of 16 weeks.

On February 21, 1982 the open interest was 40,261 and the spot price of silver was $14.57 per troy ounce. On June 19, 1989 the open interest of 87,582 had more than doubled while the price of silver kept falling to $5.28. Doesn't this tell us the increasing size of open interest has been built up with a preponderance of short positions upon short positions, thereby, economically, driving the price per ounce down?

Some day the opposite of what happened the week of February 28, 1983 may occur. Then, if the above theorem has merit and we find a significant decline in open interest accompanied by a sharp increase in price, will this portend a turnaround in the long downtrend in silver? Then, after a significant number of the short positions have been covered and a preponderance of initiation of new long positions occur, a new bull market in silver may be under way.

SELLING FUTURES CONTRACTS SHORT

The preceding analysis of open interest suggests it is as important to consider influences that point to "shorting the market" as it is to influences that point to "going long."

When trading in the stock market many investors have inhibitions against selling short. The very nature of the difference between investing in the stock market and trading in the futures market dictates giving the same weight to selling short as to buying long.

Two distinct impedimenta exist with respect to selling equities short that do not apply in futures trading. First, in selling stocks short an "uptick" in price over the last previous trade is required. Second, any dividends paid on a stock while it is held "short" must be borne by the holder of the short position.

There is a third kind of action that can prove devastating to the holder of a short position in an equity. It is when a takeover of a stock is rumored, and higher and higher bids for the company occur. The price of the stock then often rises dramatically with huge losses sustained by the short sellers.

The nearest thing to the above that could happen in the futures market would be when a commodity is being cornered, as was tried years ago with silver. Today these occurrences have all but vanished. Furthermore, the practice of placing stop-loss orders and buy-stop orders protects, to a degree, the trader in commodities.

An exception to the stop order that at least somewhat protects the trader is when, on any given day, the price of the commodity opens with a huge down-gap or a limit down day occurs. When the latter occurs, those holding long positions cannot sell them *at any price*. This can quickly produce a human reaction of utter helplessness and despair.

CUTTING LOSSES SHORT AND LETTING GAINS RUN

There is an old adage on Wall Street that says: "Cut losses short and let profits run." To do this, we should add: "At the outset of every futures trade, a stop-loss order should be placed, and for every increasingly profitable trade, higher and higher buy-stop orders should be entered."

Commodity traders should consider placing stop-loss orders at a dollar amount of, say, 5% to 10% of the amount of the margin requirement. The trader in commodities *must*, repeat, *must* be prepared to sustain many losing trades. If the trader cannot psychologically accept a run of several or more consecutive losing trades, he or she should avoid futures trading. In profitable trades letting profits run can result in considerable gains; however, if the price should reverse itself, it is essential to automatically closeout the trade by using a buy-stop order.

Unlike in the stock market where a margin of 50% is required and interest is chargeable on the unpaid balance, the margin on futures trades can run anywhere from 5% to 15%, and no interest is charged on the balance. There have been rare occasions, however, when a commodity exchange, because of wild speculative surges in prices concomitant with a huge volume of trades, has increased the margin requirements to as high as 100%.

Let's assume "normal" trading conditions are extant and a trader in gold contracts limits his losses to, say, 8% of his margin requirement by placing stop-loss orders. If the margin requirement of a gold contract is $5,000, representing 100 troy ounces of gold with the price at $400 per ounce, the money down leverage is 8 to 1. The stop-loss order would then be placed at $396 (8% stop-loss × $5,000 equals $400 stop-loss, divided by 100 ounces equals a stop at $4 under the purchased price, or at $396).

Assume three trades similar to the above are made with stop-losses equalling $1,200 (plus commissions, which are payable only when the trades are closed, as contrasted with the commissions paid on both purchases and sales of stocks).

Now consider the results if a futures contract in gold is made at $350 an ounce, and subsequently, a labor strike by gold miners is started in South Africa and soon spreads to America, Canada, and Australia. The price of gold rises rapidly to $390 per ounce. The trader, following the dictum of letting profits run, has placed higher and higher buy-stop orders, the latest of which was at $385. The price keeps rising, going from $390 to $395, and the buy-stop is raised to $390. Then the price suddenly drops to $388. The trader may only be able to receive the next trade price below $390 in a "fast" market.

Assuming the trader received a close-trade price of $388, his profit would be $3,800 ($388 minus $350 × 100).

NOTE: Many individuals engaged in futures trading may find it difficult to place buy-stop orders when they see profits ready for plucking. A natural tendency is to latch onto profits believing that "a bird in the hand is worth two in the bush" and you never go broke taking a profit. However, it should be remembered that you *can* go broke taking many small losses and making fewer small profits.

MONEY MANAGEMENT

Money management is an important strategic consideration in futures trading. Many brokerage and commodity houses have established a minimum net worth requirement before a futures trading account may be opened. Other firms require a monetary deposit in addition to the margin on the contract. One of the largest brokerage firms requires a deposit of $20,000 in a money market account in addition to the margin. Thereafter, all transactions to be paid for are deducted from the money market fund and proceeds are deposited in the fund. Interest is paid on the fund balance, and it is higher than bank rates.

In managing money it seems pertinent to determine which specific contract amongst each group of, say, agricultural, precious metals, or livestock, contracts provides the largest possible leverage for profit (or loss). Because of the desirability of trading only in contracts with high open interest, the comparative analysis discussed here should be limited to contracts with high open interest.

Contracts generally having the higher open interest amongst agricultural products are corn, world sugar, soybeans, and soybean oil; amongst livestock are cattle and pork bellies; and amongst precious metals are gold and silver.

In order to ascertain the relative leverage of contracts in each industry category, only three bits of information are generally required: the margin requirement, the price of the contract, and the number of units in a contract. The dollar margin requirement is obtainable from any commodity broker, and the other data are found in financial publications, including *Barron's*.

The following table shows how the comparative leverage of the gold and silver contracts may be determined:

	Gold	Silver
Number of troy ounces in contract	100	5,000
Multiplied by price of one December, 1989 contract	$369.40	$ 5,403
Paper Value of Contract	$36,940	$27,015
Margin requirement as of June 19, 1989	$ 2,500	$ 2,800
Basic leverage	14.78 to 1	9.64 to 1

When studying the table, note the following:

1. Higher margin requirements are generally required for spot (current) month contracts.
2. When the relative prices of two commodities usually rise and fall in tandem as do gold and silver, it might be best to trade the one with the higher leverage to obtain "the biggest bang for the buck."

Because of the extent of the above basic leverage disparity between the gold and silver contracts, no further analysis would be necessary to determine which has the greater leverage.

NOTE: A number of years ago (and for a long time) the ratio of the price of gold to silver was about 35 to 1. In recent years the ratio has been in the neighborhood of 65 to 1. In the event this ratio should drastically change by a large swing in the price of one of the metals, the above analysis could lose some or all of its validity.

In the event the basic leverage between contracts is fairly close to one another, an additional factor could be applied to determine the one with the greater leverage. The lifetime price span between the contract high and low should be determined (again from financial publications). The span of each contract would then be multiplied by its basic leverage. The resulting highest product would then be the contract with the higher leverage.

Again, it is left to the reader to make analyses similar to the above for any groupings, by industry, of interest. Such groupings might include, for instance, the leverage difference between soybeans and soybean oil, crude oil and heating oil, between corn and sugar.

Index

A

accounts receivable, aging reports, fundamental analysis of, 42-44, 66, 68

advance-decline lines, technical analysis, 8-9, 11, 34

aging reports, accounts receivable, fundamental analysis of, 42-44, 66, 68

American Electric Power Corp., 84

American Stock Exchange, xiv

annual rates, 104-105, 110

annualized rates, 104-105, 110

Arms Index, 84-85, 115-116

Arms, Richard W., Jr., 115

assets
  current, working capital ratio and fundamental analysis, 40-42
  fixed, fundamental analysis of, 44
  net, fundamental analysis of, 44-45

at-the-money options, 123

average cost method, cost of goods sold, 48

B

balance sheets
  fundamental analysis of, 40-41
  percent return on equity and, 101, 108-109

Baraurch, Bernard, 11

Barron's Weekly, 2, 39, 140

bear markets, 22-23

Bellwether Theory, GM stock, technical analysis, 29, 34

bonds, callable provisions, 81-83

book value, 64
  percent return on equity and, 99-101

Boston Traveler, 3

buy signals
  discount rate turnarounds, 5-8, 34
  Dow Theory, 5-8, 34
  price vs. volume trends, 18
  value rating of, 2, 34-35

buy-sell ratio, insiders, technical analysis, 21-22, 34

143

About the Author

Harold Wilson was employed in Wall Street in 1929. On October 28th of that year he witnessed first-hand the greatest crash in Wall Street's history. He remembers too well that awesome period of chaos and despair. Mr. Wilson recalls having walked, on many following days, down that narrow canyon of Wall Street with his eyes and head tilted upwards in fear of being struck by a falling body. This caution, he felt, was justified as evidenced by the blood-stained walls of the Equitable building, which bore mute testamony of that tragic period in history.

Mr. Wilson now lives very comfortably in retirement in a town house on a golf course in upstate New York. Most of his material well-being he attributes to investing in the stock market and in real estate, and when, among other signals, he senses "greed" setting in, he gets out of the stock market.

OTHER BESTSELLERS OF RELATED INTEREST

IMPORT/EXPORT: How to Get Started in International Trade—Carl A. Nelson

This excellent starter guide is for anyone who wants to get in on the excitement, the prestige, and the profits of doing business around the world. Nelson relates real-life success stories and proven tips, including his 20 keys to success. You'll find all you need to turn your entrepreneurial spirit into a fascinating and profitable business. 208 pages, 53 illustrations. Book No. 30052, $14.95 paperback only

SWISS BANK ACCOUNTS: A Personal Guide to Ownership, Benefits, and Use—Michael Arthur Jones

There's a real misconception about Swiss bank accounts: everyone thinks they're only for rich people and criminals. This book is a complete guide to the *uses and benefits* of Swiss bank accounts, by a respected professor of finance and authority on the subject. It's a practical manual that shows readers how to choose, open, use, and maintain an account. All procedures are highlighted with sample forms, documents, and even sample correspondence. 230 pages. Book No. 30046, $21.95 hardcover only

UNDERSTANDING WALL STREET— 2nd Edition—Jeffrey B. Little and Lucien Rhodes

"An excellent introduction to stock market intricacies"
—American Library Association Booklist

This bestselling guide to understanding and investing on Wall Street has been completely updated to reflect the most current developments in the stock market. The substantial growth of mutual funds, the emergence of index options, the sweeping new tax bill, and how to keep making money after the market reaches record highs and lows are a few of the things explained in this long awaited revision. 240 pages, 18 illustrations. Book No. 30020, $9.95 paperback, $19.95 hardcover

EXPORTING—FROM START TO FINANCE
—L. Fargo Wells and Karin B. Dulat

"In my thirty-five years of export experience this is the first book that was really helpful and answers some difficult questions." **—Ralph H. Chew,** National Federation of Export Associations and Chew International Group

Highly acclaimed by experts in international trade, this new book offers you everything you need to know to start a new export operation or improve an existing one. 460 pages. Book No. 30040. $39.95 hardcover only

COACHING FOR IMPROVED WORK PERFORMANCE—Ferdinand F. Fournies

". . . a sorely needed guide/help book for salesmarketing managers." **—The Sales Executive**

Over 70,000 copies sold in hardcover; now available for the first time in paperback! By one of the nation's best-known business training consultants and specialist in coaching procedures, this book shows you face-to-face coaching procedures that allow you to obtain immediate, positive results with your subordinates. Filled with examples, case studies, and practical problem-solving techniques. 224 pages. Book No. 30054, $12.95 paperback only

INSTANT LEGAL FORMS: Ready-to-Use Documents for Almost Any Occasion—Ralph E. Troisi

By following the clear instructions provided in this book, you can write your own will, lend or borrow money or personal property, buy or sell a car, rent out a house or apartment, check your credit, hire contractors, and grant power of attorney— all without the expense or complication of a lawyer. Author-attorney Ralph E. Troisi supplies ready-to-use forms and step-by-step guidance in filling them out and modifying them to meet your specific needs. 224 pages, Illustrated. Book No. 30028, $15.95 paperback only

Prices Subject to Change Without Notice.

Look for These and Other TAB Books at Your Local Bookstore

To Order Call Toll Free 1-800-822-8158
(in PA, AK, and Canada call 717-794-2191)

or write to TAB BOOKS, Blue Ridge Summit, PA 17294-0840.

Title	Product No.	Quantity	Price

☐ Check or money order made payable to TAB BOOKS

Charge my ☐ VISA ☐ MasterCard ☐ American Express

Acct. No. _____ Exp. _____

Signature: _____

Name: _____

Address: _____

City: _____

State: _____ Zip: _____

Subtotal $ _____

Postage and Handling
($3.00 in U.S., $5.00 outside U.S.) $ _____

Add applicable state and local
sales tax $ _____

TOTAL $ _____

TAB BOOKS catalog free with purchase; otherwise send $1.00 in check or money order and receive $1.00 credit on your next purchase.

Orders outside U.S. must pay with international money order in U.S. dollars.

TAB Guarantee: If for any reason you are not satisfied with the book(s) you order, simply return it (them) within 15 days and receive a full refund. **BC**